Praise for Collaborative Inquiry for Educators

"Donohoo provides a practical and powerful four-step process to guide collaborative inquiry teams in identifying, inventing, and investigating solutions to problems of practice that occur in their everyday work. The tools, examples, and detailed guidelines provide teacher leaders, coaches, principals, and others with the resources they need to transform unproductive team meetings into evidence-based interactions and study that result in improved practice and results for students."

—Joellen Killion, Senior Advisor, Learning Forward

"Donohoo has provided a rare gift in a book that one can read forward, backward, or in the middle. You can pinpoint your need, save time, and make immediate use of this excellent resource. The references are extensive and current. At the back of the book the reader finds eleven enormously practical and immediately applicable resources—analytical frameworks and thought-provoking questions that you can use the first time you read the text. The chapters include compelling evidence and practical advice, but it's too easy for readers to dismiss the last pages of a book. Don't make that mistake with this immensely useful and practical volume."

—Douglas Reeves, Founder,
The Center for Successful Leadership

"Collaborative Inquiry for Educators *provides a balance of conceptual knowledge and pragmatic next steps. Perfect for a grade-level or department chair."*

—Thomas Van Soelen, Associate Superintendent,
City Schools of Decatur, and
National Facilitator, School Reform Initiative

"Jenni Donohoo's book articulates in detail what facilitation needs to look like, along with how to create the conditions to actually make it happen. It is a must read for anyone trying to actively develop and support the link between teacher and leader actions, and positive student outcomes."

—Steven Katz, Director, Aporia Consulting Ltd.

"Collaborative Inquiry for Educators *is a guide for school leaders who long to move beyond superficial group meetings and into meaningful inquiry that effects actual changes in instruction and student achievement. It provides a timely guide to meeting the expectations of Common Core Standards."*

—Judy Beemer, Literacy Coach and
AVID Coordinator, Junction City High School, KS

"Often educational organizations engage in 'hot topic' practices, but not always with knowledge of how to effectively do so. Jenni Donohoo provides very clear and explicit grounding for an individual who might be assigned as a facilitator for a collaborative inquiry within a school system. In the spirit of collaborative inquiry, Donohoo recognizes the need for adaptation to different situations and often provides options for facilitators to consider. Grounding this work in the professional learning literature, she does an excellent job of weaving citations from that literature into a guiding manual for how to proceed. I would certainly recommend this resource to facilitators of or participants in a collaborative inquiry as well as to administrators who set up the opportunities for such collaborations."

—Marian Small, Dean Emerita,
University of New Brunswick, Canada

"This book provides detailed, practical, and well-grounded ideas for those wanting to make professional learning communities work effectively. It's a fine resource for anyone working with school development or improvement."

—Ben Levin, Professor and
Canada Research Chair, Leadership, Higher and
Adult Education, OISE, University of Toronto

"This book provides a practical, easy-to-follow overview of collaborative inquiry for teams of classroom teachers. No longer do you need to force a match between your school and someone else's research, now your teachers can conduct their own authentic research."

—Charre Todd, Science Teacher, Crossett Middle School, AR

"This book is an excellent hands-on manual that will guide administrators, teachers and potential administrators through the process of collaborative inquiry. This is a very practical guide to the process, with numerous vignettes making the process very easy to understand. If you have a desire to begin the process of collaborative inquiry in your school, I would definitely recommend this book."

—Stephen Armstrong, President-Elect,
National Council for the Social Studies

COLLABORATIVE
INQUIRY
for Educators

To Jim—for all of our hot tub conversations.

COLLABORATIVE INQUIRY

for Educators

A Facilitator's Guide to School Improvement

JENNI DONOHOO

CORWIN
A SAGE Company

CORWIN
A SAGE Company

FOR INFORMATION:

Corwin
A SAGE Company
2455 Teller Road
Thousand Oaks, California 91320
(800) 233-9936
www.corwin.com

SAGE Publications Ltd.
1 Oliver's Yard
55 City Road
London EC1Y 1SP
United Kingdom

SAGE Publications India Pvt. Ltd.
B 1/I 1 Mohan Cooperative Industrial Area
Mathura Road, New Delhi 110 044
India

SAGE Publications Asia-Pacific Pte. Ltd.
3 Church Street
#10-04 Samsung Hub
Singapore 049483

Acquisitions Editor: Dan Alpert
Associate Editor: Kimberly Greenberg
Editorial Assistant: Heidi Arndt
Production Editors: Cassandra Margaret
    Seibel and Melanie Birdsall
Copy Editor: Codi Bowman
Typesetter: C&M Digitals (P) Ltd.
Proofreader: Annie Lubinsky
Indexer: Jean Casalegno
Cover Designer: Karine Hovsepian
Permissions Editor: Karen Ehrmann

Printed in the United States of America

Library of Congress Cataloging-in-Publication Data

Donohoo, Jenni.

Collaborative inquiry for educators: a facilitator's guide to school improvement / Jenni Donohoo.

pages cm
Includes bibliographical references and index.

ISBN 978-1-4522-7441-6 (pbk. : alk. paper)

1. Professional learning communities. 2. Group work in education—United States. 3. Team learning approach in education—United States. 4. Educational evaluation—United States. 5. Reflective teaching. 6. School improvement programs—United States. I. Title.

LB1731.D588 2014
371.2'07—dc23   2013004677

This book is printed on acid-free paper.

SFI Certified Sourcing
www.sfiprogram.org
SFI-00453

17 10 9 8 7 6 5 4

Contents

Resources

Preface

All students deserve an education where they are appropriately challenged in an environment where teaching and learning are visible. They come to us, however, with a variety of diverse learning needs, readiness levels, background knowledge, learning preferences, and dispositions making it difficult for teachers to positively affect their learning. Together, educators can ensure greater success for *all* students by developing their knowledge, skills, and competencies based on identified student learning needs. Collaboratively, educators can learn about different approaches, identify strategies to test, assess their impact, and adjust their practices accordingly. Collaborative inquiry provides a structure for professional learning in which teachers and administrators come together to inquire, seek and share learning, collect and reflect on evidence, and act on what they have learned.

Stoll (2010) described collaborative inquiry as a means in which learning communities "deconstruct knowledge through joint reflection and analysis, re-constructing it through collaborative action, and co-constructing it through collective learning from their experiences" (p. 474). Collaborative inquiry is a process that engages educators in examining and reflecting on the link between the actions of teachers and school leaders and the outcomes of students. The four-stage model outlined in this book includes framing a problem, collecting evidence, analyzing evidence, and documenting, sharing, and celebrating. As teams cycle through the stages, they develop competencies and shared understandings of new practices. Together, they consider the impact of their actions as they examine evidence of student learning and alter instruction appropriately.

To achieve success for *all* students, there needs to be a concerted move from individual to collaborative learning. This book has been designed to support facilitators in leading school teams through a formal process of collaborative inquiry. The role of facilitator can be assumed by those in informal or formal leadership positions. It does not matter whether the facilitator is an administrator, teacher, staff developer, or coach. What does matter is that the facilitator takes deliberate action in leading teams through the process. Intentional facilitation is required to ensure that the work is purposeful, productive, and impactful. By following the systematic approach outlined in this resource, facilitators will gain a better understanding of the stages of collaborative inquiry and how to implement it as a powerful design for professional learning and a high-leverage strategy for school improvement.

In this book, facilitators will find activities that are designed to do the following:

- Ensure that teams focus on the *right work* by identifying common issues that stem from current student learning needs and that are aligned with larger school improvement efforts
- Elicit action through the identification and implementation of evidence-based practices that address issues directly related to improving the learning for students in schools
- Develop teachers' competencies and shared understandings of new practices
- Initiate and support productive conversations that challenge beliefs in respectful ways
- Lead to continuous improvement, self-sustaining teams, and changes in existing practice

This book also provides vignettes and examples throughout.

As the process unfolds, the critical role of reflection in enabling participants to adapt to changes will become apparent to facilitators. As such, facilitators are encouraged to reflect on their practice as well as they guide teams through each stage of collaborative inquiry. Looking inward and reflecting on the practice of facilitation will help facilitators to sharpen their personal capacity to lead change. At the end of each stage, facilitators will find a list of skills and approaches for effective facilitation and are encouraged to self-assess in an effort to identify strengths and consider areas for development.

For systemic change to occur, opportunities for teachers to lead and to learn from one another need to be provided. Collaborative inquiry is a powerful design as it recognizes the role of teachers in ongoing school improvement. Facilitators of professional learning can use this resource as a guide to employing structured collaborative learning experiences for educators that are grounded in their current problems of practice. Introducing collaborative inquiry into the work of professional learning communities will help to ingrain a culture of inquiry and reflection within the school. When educators learn from one another, solutions to problems are generated through collaborative discussions and personal reflections. These learning opportunities help build leadership and spread good ideas and practices throughout the system.

Acknowledgments

I 've been privileged to work with a number of teams at the Greater Essex County District School Board over the course of my career. Engaging in academic conversations with dedicated members of professional learning communities including department heads, teachers, administrators, and coaches has shaped my thoughts and ideas. Participating in rich discussions about school improvement with consultants and senior administrators has influenced my thinking as well.

I have benefited greatly from collaborating with educators through professional networks including Learning Forward, the Ontario Principals' Council, School Board University Research Exchange, Managing Information for Student Achievement, and EduGAINS (Growing Accessible and Interactive Networks). Working with dedicated educators from these organizations has been an honor and has helped me grow both personally and professionally.

I would like to thank Amy Lin, President of Learning Forward Ontario, for connecting me with Dan Alpert at Corwin. I would like to thank Dan for his collaborative approach and support throughout the publishing process.

I would also like to thank my husband, Jim, for his patience and assistance during the drafting, revising, and editing of this work.

PUBLISHER'S ACKNOWLEDGMENTS

Corwin gratefully acknowledges the contributions of the following reviewers:

Stephen Armstrong
President-Elect
National Council for the
  Social Studies
Washington, DC

Judy Beemer
JCHS Literacy Coach and
  AVID Coordinator
Junction City, KS

Nancy Betler
Talent Development Facilitator
Charlotte Mecklenburg
  Schools
Charlotte, NC

Michelle Gayle
K–12 District Administrator—
  Teaching and Learning
Leon County School District
Tallahassee, FL

Beverly Ginther
Staff Development
  Coordinator (retired)
Minnetonka, MN

Susan Leeds
Educator
Howard Middle School
Orlando, FL

Rosetta Riddle
Professional Learning
  Coordinator
Henry County Schools
McDonough, GA

Christina M. Smith
Social Studies Department Chair
Algonquin Regional High School
Northborough, MA

Charre Todd
Science Teacher
Crossett Middle School
Crossett, AR

Marian White-Hood
Director of Academics
Maya Angelou Public
  Charter School
Washington, DC

About the Author

Photo by John Lucassian

Jenni Donohoo is a Research and Program Evaluation Consultant with the Greater Essex County District School Board. Jenni holds a doctorate in education from the University of Windsor, Brock University, and Lakehead University's Joint Educational Studies PhD Program. Her classroom teaching experiences include elementary, secondary, and post-secondary education.

In her role, supporting system leaders in developing professional learning communities, Jenni has promoted collaborative inquiry as a viable approach to system improvement for years. While serving as the President of Learning Forward Ontario, Jenni designed a program that immersed educators in the collaborative inquiry process so that they could experience it and, in turn, facilitate teams back in their schools and districts. She also helped to design a course on facilitating collaborative inquiry for the Ontario Principals' Council.

Jenni believes that collaboration and reflection are essential elements in developing formal and informal leadership in schools and that leadership development and peer-to-peer collaboration are key to sustaining meaningful changes in practice.

Jenni lives in Amherstburg, Ontario, with her husband, Jim, and their two golden retrievers, Tilley and Taylor.

1

Why Collaborative Inquiry?

Powerful professional learning designs provide the activities that make professional learning communities more than just a structure.

(Easton, 2008, p. 4)

Everyday educators face a variety of challenges. Some challenges are *technical* in nature while others are *adaptive* in nature. Technical challenges are ones in which the problem is clear, the knowledge and capacity to solve the issue already resides in the expertise of individuals, and solutions and implementation are readily understood. In education, a technical solution entails doing things we already know how to do—for example, increasing the penalty for late or missing work. A problem arises when doing what has always been done is not the right thing to do or does not result in the outcomes intended. An adaptive challenge is "one for which the necessary knowledge to solve the problem does not yet exist" (Vander Ark, 2006, p. 10). Adaptive challenges are more difficult to resolve as solutions and implementation require new learning and upset past ways of doing things—for example, raising awareness of ineffective grading practices. To tackle adaptive challenges, individuals must adopt new values and beliefs.

Heifetz, Grashow, and Linsky (2009) noted that when individuals and organizations meet adaptive challenges, they themselves become something different—they adapt. Change of this magnitude is not easily accomplished, as people's ideas about how things work are not easily reconstructed. By focusing efforts on professional learning approaches

"The definition of insanity is doing the same thing over and over and expecting different results." (Benjamin Franklin)

The adaptive challenges educators face vary in their nature and complexity. Educators might be grappling with one or more of the following issues:

- Supporting English Language Learners
- Closing the gap between groups of students in the areas of literacy and numeracy
- Accommodating students with learning disabilities
- Improving graduation rates
- Accessing background knowledge when working with groups of diverse students

Whatever student needs are identified, the challenge of change is "compounded by pressure from others to remain the same" (Levin, 2008, p. 81). Levin noted that effective change in schools comes from "thoughtful application of effective practices in particular contexts" (p. 81). When doing what has been done does not result in outcomes intended, real change is required. Real change comes and is sustained when goals are achieved in new ways under complex circumstances. When real change occurs, students and educators benefit.

that challenge mental models and engaging people in learning and working collaboratively, individuals and organizations will be more likely to meet adaptive challenges. Collaborative inquiry is a structure in which members of a professional learning community (PLC) come together to systematically examine their educational practices. Teams work together to ask questions, develop theories of action, determine action steps, and gather and analyze evidence to assess the impact of their actions. Throughout this process, teams test presuppositions about what they think will work against the evidence of what actually works (City, Elmore, Fiarman, & Teitel, 2009). By closely examining and reflecting on the results of their actions, individuals and teams begin to think differently. They begin to question long-standing beliefs and consider implications for their professional practices.

Leading educational researchers recognize the power of the PLC concept to transform schools and help educators meet the adaptive challenges confronting them and, therefore, continue to promote collaborative inquiry as a strategy for strengthening teaching and learning. In a study that examined specific characteristics of school improvement plans that were most related to student achievement, Reeves (2010) found that the *inquiry process* was one of nine characteristics that had a measurable and significant effect on gains in student achievement in reading and mathematics in both elementary and secondary schools. Reeves (2010) encouraged teachers to take an active role in expressing and testing hypotheses and backed the notion that collaborative inquiry can have a profound impact on the professional practices not only of the participants but of their colleagues as well. Katz, Earl, and Ben Jaafar (2009) included collaborative inquiry that challenged thinking and practice as a key component in their theory of action for enabling impactful PLCs. Supovitz (2006) noted that when members of PLCs engage together in investigating challenges of practice, their understanding of those challenges grows deeper and is more unified, practice grows more sophisticated and powerful, and the group develops a tighter sense of camaraderie and common purpose. As a result, teams can construct common understanding, share knowledge and experience, and develop common goals (Supovitz, 2006).

Teacher-driven inquiry is not a new approach. For years, Lieberman among others has promoted a culture of inquiry where teachers have opportunities to discuss, think about, try, and hone new practices through structures such as problem-solving groups or decision-making teams. Promoting a contextual and collaborative approach, Lieberman and Miller (2004) stated, "The concept of learning in practice is now viewed as foundational to teacher leadership; it rests on the idea that learning is more social, collaborative, and context-dependent than was previously thought" (p. 21).

Although it is not a new approach, collaborative inquiry is more frequently being used to address school improvement efforts. As elements of and conditions for effective professional learning are identified and better understood, educators are recognizing the potential impact that collaborative inquiry could have on sustaining changes in practice and ultimately achieving greater success for *all* students. Learning Forward (Killion, Hord, Roy, Kennedy, & Hirsh, 2012) identified standards that can be used to guide the design, implementation, and evaluation of professional learning. Under the category of "Learning Communities," Learning Forward promotes an inquiry approach stating that high-quality professional learning includes learning communities that "apply a cycle of continuous improvement to engage in inquiry, action research, data analysis, planning, implementation, reflection, and evaluation" (Killion et al., 2012, p. 16). Learning Forward also promotes a collaborative approach to learning noting, "The more one educator's learning is shared and supported by others, the more quickly the culture of continuous improvement, collective responsibility, and high expectations for students and educators grows" (p. 17). More frequently, educational leaders are engaging

> Some educators associate collaborative inquiry and action research with experimental research approaches and hesitate to participate, as they are not confident in their skills to conduct research. While collaborative inquiry is a process in which educators come together to examine their educational practices systematically using techniques of research, the intent is not for participants to focus on rigorous research designs or methodologies. Collaborative inquiry is primarily a process to support professional learning. Since it is contextual in nature, it is not expected that findings are generalized to a larger population.

practitioners in the process of inquiry, recognizing that it embodies the characteristics of high quality professional learning and valuing its potential for school improvement.

While collaborative inquiry is becoming a more commonly used professional learning model and it has been shown to be an effective approach to sustaining meaningful changes in practice, studies show that the investment does not always yield anticipated results. Katz (2010) stated that the majority of learning communities do not produce sustainable changes in professional understanding, classroom practice, or student achievement. Mitchell and Sackney (2009) suggested that PLCs "have remarkably little impact on the ways in which teachers teach, students learn, or leaders lead" (p. 12). After many observations across various settings, the researchers concluded that "deep, rich, authentic learning promised by learning community discourse" (p. 9) was evident in only a small number of high-capacity schools. Fullan (2006) also noted that it was common for communities to be operating on a superficial level.

As the adaptive nature of this work unfolds, facilitators face challenges in their efforts to embed collaborative inquiry into the work of PLCs in a way that is purposeful, productive, and impactful. DuFour, DuFour, Eaker, and Karhanek (2010) noted that one of the most common mistakes educators make as they attempt to implement PLC concepts is to regard collaboration as the end itself, rather than as a means to an end. They noted that collaboration would impact student achievement in a positive way only if collective inquiry focused on the right work. Easton (2008) warned, "Without meaningful learning activities that occur during PLC time, PLCs may go the way of so many other structures that were instituted without any attention to what teachers and students do that would take advantage of those structures" (p. 4). This book answers the question for leaders of educational change: *How can I facilitate teams through the stages of collaborative inquiry while ensuring the work is purposeful, productive, and impactful?*

A FOUR-STAGE MODEL

This resource has been designed for facilitators interested in guiding school teams through a formal process of inquiry. It is of increasing importance to support individuals and teams through the change process, as collaborative inquiry requires people to think, reflect, and work together in new ways. Simply providing time for teachers' growth opportunities is not enough. The tools to support meaningful collaboration that is focused on what matters most—identifying and addressing the learning needs of students—are needed as well. To ensure the integrity of the design so that greater success for *all* students can be realized, it is imperative that facilitators develop a deep understanding of how to support teams through the process. The four-stage model outlined in this book complete with the insights, suggestions, and prompts, will provide facilitators with what they need to guide teams so that the efforts of the team make a difference for the students they serve.

The four-stage model includes the following:

Stage 1: Framing the Problem. During this stage, facilitators assist teams as they determine a meaningful focus, develop an inquiry about a particular link between professional practices and student results, and formulate a theory of action.

Stage 2: Collecting Evidence. In the second stage, facilitators guide teams in developing shared understandings and building additional knowledge and competencies. Teams determine the type of evidence to collect. They also determine when, where, and how it will be collected.

Stage 3: Analyzing Evidence. Once teams feel they have gathered enough information to address the question posed, facilitators guide teams through a five-step approach to analyzing evidence. Teams learn how to make meaning of data by identifying patterns and themes and formulating conclusions. As teams refine their thinking, they revisit their theory of action accordingly.

Stage 4: Documenting, Sharing, and Celebrating. During this final stage, teams come together to document, share, and celebrate their new understandings. Teams consider next steps by identifying additional student learning needs and reflecting on what they learned through their inquiries. Finally, teams debrief the process by considering how their work was reflective of the characteristics of collaborative inquiry.

Once facilitators engage teams in collaborative inquiry, they will find it is a more cyclical than linear model. Teams cycle through the stages, revisiting each stage as they change and refine their thinking.

> The four stages of collaborative inquiry (framing the problem, collecting evidence, examining evidence, and documenting, sharing, and celebrating) are the same stages used in action research. The difference between the two approaches is that collaborative inquiry is conducted by a group of educators interested in addressing a school, department, division, or common classroom issue driven by student learning needs. The work is often connected to a broader district and/or school improvement strategy. Action research is conducted by individuals and a single classroom is more often the unit for improvement.

GETTING STARTED

In preparing to lead teams, there are a few things for facilitators to consider. For example, facilitators need to consider issues regarding timing, including when to begin and the length of the cycle of inquiry. When forming a collaborative inquiry team considerations include optimal size, participants, and recruitment strategies. In addition, facilitators should consider ways to foster academic discourse. These ideas are expanded on in the section that follows.

Timing

When is the best time during the school year to begin? How long might it take to complete a cycle? These are some commonly asked questions as people prepare to get started. If the work is going to be connected to larger improvement efforts, the best time to introduce collaborative inquiry is when the process of school improvement planning takes place. In many school districts, school improvement planning begins in the last month of the previous school year—projecting ahead for the year to come. Some school districts wait until the current school year begins to conduct a comprehensive needs assessment. In any case, if collaborative inquiry is going to be used as a structure to guide school improvement efforts, the two processes must begin simultaneously to complement each other. By introducing collaborative inquiry as a strategy for school improvement, it will help team members understand how it relates to the work that is already happening in schools.

The length of the cycle will depend on the team, the question, the school year calendar, and structural conditions. For teams new to the process, it may take longer to complete a cycle than it would for teams who have experienced it before. It is similar to when teachers introduce a new strategy to students. Initially, students' cognitive energy is spent processing how to use the strategy. Once they become familiar with how the strategy works, they are able to focus cognitive energy on the content and advance their learning. Once collaborative inquiry teams get used to the stages and engage in one full cycle, they will be able to use their time more efficiently. The length of the cycle will also depend on the question posed. Questions that identify a change in classroom practice that requires a steep learning curve for participating teachers will increase the length of time the team engages in professional learning and the implementation of strategies in the classroom. A skilled facilitator will ensure that the practices identified are high-leverage while scaffolding learning accordingly so that team members feel safe in the learning environment. The length of the cycle will also depend on the school year calendar. Facilitators should be aware of the start and end dates of terms when working with teams in schools that operate in a semester system. Ideally, cycles should be completed during a single semester. Finally, the length of time to complete a cycle will also depend on supportive structural conditions. Hord (2008) described supportive structural conditions as "those such as time to meet, a place to meet, and policies and resources that support the staff coming together for study and learning" (p. 12). Teams will be most productive if supported and provided with time embedded in their daily practice to engage in the work.

Forming a Collaborative Inquiry Team

Collaborative inquiry teams may comprise as few as two educators. Teams ranging from five to seven participants are ideal. When teams consist of more than seven people, facilitators might find it challenging to ensure that all voices are heard. In addition, depending on the makeup of the team, the larger the team becomes, the more difficult it may be to identify a common student learning need. However, larger teams may work as long as the individuals coming together are able to identify a school, department, or division issue driven by the consideration of common and current student learning needs.

Identifying informal leaders who are open to sharing their practice and who have the ability to engage and motivate other staff is important. Katz et al. (2009) suggested that formal leaders "distribute leadership, identifying those teacher leaders who are in the position to lead in a focus area because of their expertise" (p. 75). Additionally, the collaborative inquiry team should consist of individuals who are able to take action and who are willing to engage in and promote an inquiry approach to professional learning in their schools, departments, or divisions.

When recruiting individuals, facilitators might consider the idea of "starting with why" proposed by Sinek (2009). Sinek suggested that for leaders to inspire action, they need to start with *why* rather than *how* or *what*. While *what* people do serves as proof of what they believe, *why* they do it represents their purpose and beliefs. Consider the following two approaches. In the first example, the facilitator's recruitment script begins with *what*, while in the second approach, the recruitment strategy begins with *why*.

Example 1

WHAT—"This year, teachers will conduct collaborative inquiry while participating in a professional learning community."

HOW—"Forty minutes a week will be structured into your schedule. Teachers in the same division will share common time in which they will come together to investigate an issue stemming from an identified common student learning need."

WHY—"As a result of our collaboration, we will all be better equipped to address the learning needs of our students." (Donohoo, 2012)

Example 2

WHY—"I believe that students deserve the very best education but they come to us with gaps in their understanding and that makes it difficult and challenging for educators to meet the diverse needs of all learners."

HOW—"We can work together to identify the gaps in our knowledge based on identified student learning needs. Collaboratively, we can learn about different approaches, identify strategies to test them, assess their impact, and revise them accordingly."

WHAT—"Collaborative inquiry is an approach for teacher development and learning and it provides a structure where teachers and administrators come together to continuously seek and share learning and then act on what they have learned."

Sinek (2009) suggested that great and inspiring leaders appeal to people's emotions and inspire action by starting with purposes, causes, or beliefs rather than describing the *what*. Heath and Heath (2010) also noted that in successful change efforts, leaders speak in ways that influence emotions and not with analytical arguments. Since people are motivated by emotions, starting with *why* will prove to be an effective recruitment strategy for facilitators when forming collaborative inquiry teams.

In addition, team members should be made aware of the commitment of time and energy that will be required throughout the process. When recruiting individuals, it is important to share with potential team members an overview of the four stages of collaborative inquiry along with the estimated length of time involved so that they know what is expected of them. Some individuals may be hesitant to commit but for those who do agree to participate, having clear expectations will lead to the creation of a healthier and more productive team.

Fostering Academic Discourse

MacDonald (2011) described a "culture of nice" as the "underlying culture that inhibits the team from reaching a level of rigorous collaborative discourse where teachers are challenging each other's and their own thinking, beliefs, assumptions, and practice" (p. 45). The author pointed out that "teachers must be willing to expose their struggles and failures with their colleagues, and colleagues must be willing to tell the truth, or teams will go through the motions of collaborative inquiry but never see results" (p. 45). When facilitators enter into this process, they must be prepared to foster academic discourse that shifts from a culture of nice so that team members can gain insights into their practices and results for students can be realized.

To produce meaningful change, facilitators need to provide opportunities for teams to respectfully discuss differences between beliefs within the organization. It is difficult and challenging work. Fullan (2011) pointed out that adaptive challenges and social complexity are one and the same, noting, "It is not that the problem is mysterious; it is more that helping people discover and embrace change is socially complex" (p. 18). At times, discussions will make people feel uncomfortable, but it is necessary to engage in difficult conversations. Facilitators can begin by valuing and acknowledging that people have different ways of interpreting things. Encouraging team members to listen with curiosity and not judgment will help people to engage in conversations in respectful ways. When discussing classroom practices and/or student work, facilitators should ensure that participants provide descriptions rather than offering interpretations. City et al. (2009) noted that to talk to one another productively about what we see in classrooms, we have to describe what we see "without the heavy judgmental overlay that we typically bring" (p. 87). Specific descriptions provided about classroom practices and/or student work will give participants an enormous amount of information to reflect on in terms of their practice. If the facilitator is not prepared to foster these types of conversations, the time spent engaging in the process is unlikely to result in sustained changes in practice.

Activities and prompts contained in this book have been designed to assist facilitators in structuring conversations so that people's assumptions are safely challenged. Focusing conversation on evidence rather than opinion, providing opportunities for all voices to be heard, and promoting reflection on professional practices will help facilitators shift the culture from "nice" to a more honest discourse where results can be realized.

Senge (1990) used the term "learning organizations" to describe organizations that transformed themselves to meet adaptive challenges and become knowledge-generating versus merely knowledge-using organizations. Vander Ark (2006) noted that meeting an adaptive challenge required "creating the knowledge and tools to solve the problem in the act of working on it" (p. 10). To shape an organization that can generate the knowledge to meet adaptive challenges, system leaders must provide opportunities for teams of learners to engage in inquiry, develop and apply theories of action, collect and analyze relevant data, reflect on practice, determine next steps and actions, and evaluate the process. Collaborative inquiry provides the structure for teams to collaboratively generate knowledge while investigating problems of practice. This book was developed to guide facilitators in leading teams in meeting adaptive challenges. A systematic approach to conducting collaborative inquiry is outlined in the chapters that follow.

Stage 1

Framing the Problem

Unlike a technical problem, there is no clear, linear path to the resolution of an adaptive challenge. You need a plan, but you also need freedom to deviate from the plan as new discoveries emerge, as conditions change, and as new forms of resistance arise.

(Heifetz, Grashow, & Linsky, 2009, p. 31)

During the first stage of collaborative inquiry, teams determine a meaningful focus, develop an inquiry question, and formulate a theory of action. Contained in this chapter are scaffolded activities facilitators can use to guide participants through each of these processes.

DETERMINING A MEANINGFUL FOCUS

Identifying an area on which to focus the team's inquiry is the first step in the process. The most effective collaborative inquiry teams keep in mind that their end goal is to increase learning and achieve greater success for *all* students. To support the team in achieving this goal, facilitators must ensure that the team considers certain criteria while determining a meaningful focus.

A well-framed problem meets the following criteria:

- Is based on identified, current student learning needs
- Is connected to a shared vision
- Addresses an issue individuals can act on and
- Is manageable for the team

Beginning by identifying current student learning needs will help ensure that the inquiry is authentic, relevant, and worth the investment. DuFour, DuFour, Eaker, and Karhanek (2010) note, "Collaboration would impact student achievement in a positive way only if the 'co-labouring' and collective inquiry focused on the *right* work" (p. 33). It is important in the first stage that teams take the time to identify the knowledge, skills, and competencies that students need to develop. As the process unfolds, teams use this information as a basis for examining *their* professional practices, identifying gaps in *their* knowledge and competencies, and determining a plan for professional learning.

There is a consensus among change theorists that collaborative efforts result in greater success when beliefs and visions are shared throughout an organization. Senge (1990) described shared vision as shared pictures of the future that foster genuine commitment and enrollment, rather than compliance to organizational goals, and "a force in people's hearts" (p. 206) that provides the focus and energy for learning. By guiding the team in articulating a shared vision, facilitators help establish a common sense of purpose and a clear picture of what success looks like among team members. This will help inspire and motivate individuals to take action.

The focus of the inquiry must also be an issue individuals can act on. Identifying promising approaches and implementing changes in practice are key elements in this process. If the problem the team identifies falls outside their realm of control, there will be little they can do to impact change. For example, if the team's answer to the question "what do many of your students experience difficulty doing?" is "getting out of bed in the morning," they will have little influence impacting immediate changes in this area. During this stage, the facilitator assists the team in identifying concerns and priorities in which they can take deliberate steps to impact change.

Finally, but not least important, the team needs to consider the scope and magnitude of the problem identified. The team must have the time and resources necessary to investigate and address the issue. Gersten, Vaughn, Deshler, and Schiller (1997) pointed out the scope and magnitude of the intended change contributes to the sustained use of interventions. If the scope and magnitude requires "radical, fundamental changes in teaching in a short period of time" (p. 469), sustained change is unlikely to occur. Therefore, it is important that the facilitator assist the team in selecting an issue that is both manageable and achievable.

The activities in this section are designed to help collaborative inquiry teams determine a meaningful focus, establish a shared vision, and consider actionable steps while ensuring manageability.

Activity 1—Identifying Student Learning Needs

> Materials Needed: Sticky Notes, Pens, Blank Chart Paper, Identifying Student Learning Needs (Resource A)

The purpose of this activity is to ensure that the focus of the team's inquiry is based on current student learning needs. Katz, Earl, and Ben Jaafar (2009) suggested,

> When it comes to establishing a focus, the goal is to identify the most urgent student learning needs by tapping into the tacit knowledge as the source of possible hypothesis. On the basis of the group's tacit knowledge, what do members think are the student learning needs and what do they think they know about the various factors that are germane to them? From there, they move to a third question—what evidence do they have (or could they get) to inform their hypothesis? (p. 29)

The following activity is designed to assist teams in identifying student learning needs to ensure that the team's inquiry is authentic, relevant, and worth the time and energy that will be required to investigate and address the issue.

Brainstorming Student Learning Needs. Provide each team member with sticky notes and ask individuals to identify and record student learning needs. Request that participants write one response per sticky note and that they work silently on their own.

> *Possible Prompts:* What are some key student learning needs? What is it that your students struggle with the most? What do many of your students experience difficulty doing?

Providing Evidence. Next, ask individuals to reflect on each need identified and provide evidence that verifies the need. Record the evidence on the same sticky note.

> *Possible Prompts:* Review the student learning needs you identified. How do you know these are needs? What is the evidence? What is it about students that caused you to believe the issues identified are needs?

The following serve as examples:

> Student Learning Need: Students experience difficulty forming and supporting an opinion.
> Evidence: Most students provide a reason for their position but they do not always provide support for their reason.
>
> Student Learning Need: Students need better problem-solving skills in mathematics.
> Evidence: Students require a lot of assistance in understanding problems and often cannot generalize their learning to new situations.
>
> Student Learning Need: Students lack the ability to provide quality, descriptive feedback to their peers.
> Evidence: Students fail to refer to learning targets and success criteria on peer assessment forms and during feedback conversations with their peers.
>
> Student Learning Need: Students experience difficulty comprehending while reading.
> Evidence: They have the ability to regurgitate, but when asked to explain what something means, they are unable to do so.

Facilitators may need to assist teams in articulating the needs in terms of *student learning*. Consider the following:

> Student Learning Need: Students need to honor due dates.
> Evidence: They don't complete their homework and turn assignments in late.
>
> Student Learning Need: Students need to contribute when working with their peers.
> Evidence: Students' lack of contribution to group work.
>
> Student Learning Need: Students need to review their notes.
> Evidence: Students are unable to recall information from the previous day's lesson.

Over the past few years in education, data-driven decision making has received increasing attention. Achievement test data have been predominantly valued as important sources of information to guide school improvement efforts. When completing this activity, facilitators should encourage participants to consider assessment information obtained through a variety of means including day-to-day observations, conversations, and student work products.

While the needs identified in these last three examples are real issues, they imply a lack of responsibility on the part of the student and seem to remove the obligation of dealing with the issues from teachers. The way they are phrased implies that the onus is on students to fix the problem. In addition, the needs identified in the previous examples are related to learning skills and work habits as opposed to the knowledge and skills students are expected to develop and demonstrate in their classwork, on tests, and in various other activities on which their achievement is assessed and evaluated. To avoid responses being phrased in such ways, facilitators may want to draw this distinction to the attention of the team prior to the brainstorming of student learning needs. One way facilitators might do so is through the sorting activity described next.

Refer to Identifying Student Learning Needs (Resource A). The items on the left illustrate student learning needs based on the Common Core State Standards. The items on the right illustrate student learning needs based on behaviors and work habits. Prepare for the team to sort these items by photocopying the cards and cutting each of them out individually.

Figure 2.1 Student Learning Needs Card Sort

Student Learning Needs Based on Common Core State Standards	**Student Learning Needs Based on Behaviors and Work Habits**
Need: Students need to develop the ability to evaluate other points of view critically and constructively. **Evidence:** They do not question texts and often take material at face value.	**Need:** Students need to stay organized. **Evidence**: They miss important dates and are unable to juggle the demands of multiple courses.
Need: Students need to improve estimation skills. **Evidence:** They cannot ballpark reasonable guesses.	**Need:** Students need to complete tasks. **Evidence:** They give up when faced with challenging problems.

Ask the team members to sort the cards into two categories without providing the titles of each category. Team members will often identify the differences between the two sets of student learning needs (knowledge and understanding versus behaviors and work habits). Once the cards are sorted, ask the team to share the reasons behind their sort and engage them in a discussion to help focus them on identifying needs that align with the Common Core State Standards.

Identifying Common Needs. Once student learning needs have been identified, to identify which need the team holds in common, facilitators lead participants in an affinity mapping exercise (National School Reform Faculty, n.d.).[1] Affinity mapping is a technique for grouping and understanding information and provides a way for teams to discuss and analyze issues. The beginning of this activity is completed in silence. Facilitators ask participants to place sticky notes containing student learning needs and evidence one at a time on the blank chart paper without talking to one another. As each sticky note is placed, other participants may place similar ideas in close proximity—organizing ideas by natural categories. The facilitator should acknowledge that it can be difficult to remain silent during this activity while reinforcing the importance that participants should resist the temptation to talk to one another while sorting and categorizing ideas.

> *Possible Prompts:* Which ideas go together? As you read what others have written, feel free to move your note and/or the notes of others so that the identified student learning needs are organized by category. Avoid the temptation to discuss categories until all sticky notes are placed on the chart paper.

Once the team has settled on the categories, have them place the sticky notes in neat columns on the chart paper. Ask them to discuss the categories and determine a label for each category (e.g., higher-level thinking skills, problem-solving skills, learning strategies).

Prioritizing. To help teams prioritize, facilitators refer to the categories generated during the affinity mapping exercise and lead an open discussion to assist the team in narrowing the focus of the inquiry.

> *Possible Prompts:* Based on the identified student learning needs, what are the priorities our team should be working on collaboratively? What additional evidence do we need to consider that will help inform our decision? Which of the priorities is the most important to us? Why? Which of the priorities is broad enough to involve most of the staff?
>
> Which of the priorities has the potential for wide impact? How are the priorities aligned with the Common Core State Standards?

DETERMINING A SHARED VISION

In examining the role that shared values and vision played in professional learning community development, Huffman (2001) noted, "The emergence of a strong, shared vision based on collective values provided the foundation for informed leadership, staff commitment, student success, and sustained school growth" (p. 18). Fullan and Sharratt (2007) note, "One condition for sustainability involves working on defining, shaping and refining the shared vision of the school" (p. 127). Holding a clear vision of success is important for collaborative inquiry teams. It will help the team determine where they are, where they want to go, and how to get there. The purpose of these activities is to ensure that the team shares a clear vision of what success looks and sounds like.

Two activities for determining a shared vision are suggested in Activities 2 and 3 (Preferred Futures and Destination Postcards). Both activities engage teams in visioning alternative futures. Senge, Scharmer, Jaworski, and Flowers (2004) noted, "Scenarios can alter people's awareness" (p. 25), and if used "artfully, people actually begin to think about a future that they've ignored or denied" (p. 25). Senge et al. (2004) also noted, "The key is to see the different future not as inevitable, but as one of several genuine possibilities" (p. 25). Facilitators are encouraged to select one activity to assist teams in describing the future they hope to achieve.

Activity 2—Preferred Futures

> Materials Needed: Paper, Pens

Earl (2003) shared the work of an Australian researcher who identified three categories of futures for education:

> "Possible Futures—things that could happen, although many of them are unlikely;
> Probable Futures—things that probably will happen, unless something is done to turn events around;
> Preferred Futures—things that you prefer to have happen and/or that you would like to happen." (Earl, 2003, p. 3)

Facilitators guide team members in developing a shared vision of a preferred future by having the group consider the top priority identified.

> *Possible Prompts:* Regarding the priorities we have identified, what are our hopes for the students we teach? If the team were to meet with success, what would the results be?
> In other words, what is our team's preferred future? If it was two years from today and we succeeded reaching our goals, what would that look like? Sound like? How would we describe our preferred future?

The following example was developed by a team of teachers whose goal was to develop students' problem-solving proficiency in mathematics. They described their preferred future this way:

> "We want to see our students become proficient problem-solvers. It isn't enough for them to gain procedural understanding; we also want them to gain conceptual understanding so that they can transfer skills from one situation to another. We want our students to have a number of strategies at their disposal and confidence in their ability to select and implement appropriate solution strategies. We want them to understand the value of approaching problems in a systematic manner and persevere when faced with difficult problems."

Activity 3—Destination Postcards

> Materials Needed: Blank Index Cards, Pens

Heath and Heath (2010) advocate using destination postcards to overcome barriers to change and note that they can be very inspiring. Destination postcards are "pictures of a future that hard work can make possible" (Heath & Heath, 2010, p. 85).

Describing the destination and determining where the team is headed helps team members appreciate why the journey is worthwhile. It also helps them consider long-term goals that will lead to provoked action and inspired effort. Facilitators guide team members in developing a destination postcard by having the group consider the top priority identified. Provide each team member with a blank index card (to serve as their destination postcard).

> *Possible Prompts:* Regarding the priorities we have identified, what are our hopes for the students we teach? If the team were to meet with success, what would the results be?
>
> In other words, what destination are we trying to reach? If it was two years from today and we succeeded reaching this destination, what would that look like? Sound like? How would we describe our final destination?

The following example was developed by a team of English teachers who wanted their students to exhibit the capacities of a literate individual as described in the Common Core Standards for English Language Arts and Literacy in History/Social Studies, Science, and Technical Subjects. The English teachers described their destination this way:

"Students are independent, self-directed learners who have mastered a broad array of reading skills. By thinking critically and creatively, they are able to assess information and solve complex problems. They communicate effectively to various audiences through various means. Students learn collaboratively and seek to understand other perspectives and cultures. They know themselves as learners and are able to build on their strengths by regulating their learning accordingly."

Next, facilitators lead a discussion. Ask the team to consider the following questions:

- Where are we right now in relation to our preferred future/destination?
- What have we tried so far to support our vision?
- What factors or obstacles have prevented us from achieving the level of success described in our preferred future/destination?

Artifact: In the final stage of collaborative inquiry, teams share their stories. Facilitators are encouraged to save documentation of the team's preferred future and/or destination postcard so that it could be considered for inclusion in the final report.

Activity 4—Sphere of Concern Versus Realm of Control

Materials Needed: Sphere of Concern Versus Realm of Control (Resource B), sticky notes

The purpose of this activity is to ensure that the concerns and priorities identified are issues that fall within the team's realm of control. Marzano (2003) offered compelling evidence regarding the profound impact of school-level and teacher-level factors on student achievement in his synthesis of educational research. Hattie's (2009) synthesis of more than 800 metaanalyses provided further insight regarding how factors outside the home including the school, curriculum, teacher, and teaching strategies influence student achievement. While contributions from the home (e.g., socioeconomic status, home environment, and parental involvement) demonstrate strong relationships with student achievement, these factors will, more often than not, fall outside the team's realm of control. It is important for facilitators to ensure that the team narrows its priorities to issues that are within their realm of control.

Identifying factors that are within the team's realm of control can be an empowering experience. It helps educators realize the extent to which they can impact the lives of students. It can lead to the development of collective efficacy and strengthen commitment by building on the common sense of purpose that was established through the team's shared vision. In moving the conversation away from factors the team has no control over, complaints are minimized. Also, through this process, team members begin to identify the action steps needed to impact change.

Figure 2.2 Sphere of Concern Versus Realm of Control

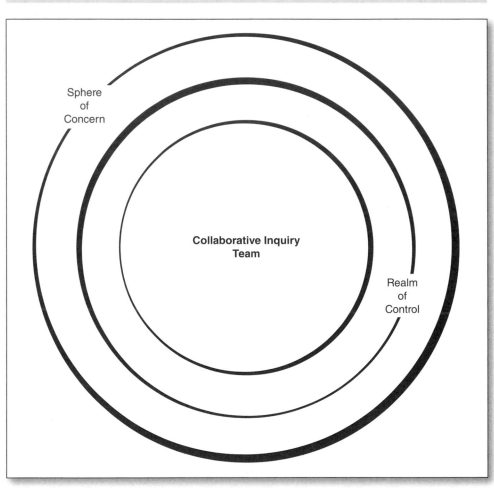

Source: National School Reform Faculty (NSRF). Created by Daniel Baron. Adapted by Jenni Donohoo. http://www.nsrfharmony.org. Reproduced with permission.

Ask your team to place themselves in the smallest center circle and imagine success lies outside all of the circles. Recording one concern per sticky note, ask the team to list all the things they are concerned about regarding the student learning needs and the priorities previously identified.

Provide teams plenty of time to ensure that the list is exhaustive, containing *all* of the team's concerns. Have team members place sticky notes in the outer ring (Sphere of Concern). Next, instruct the team to consider which issues from the outer ring they have control over. Team members move the sticky notes that identify these issues into the inside circle (Realm of Control). Ensure sufficient time to allow for careful consideration and critical thinking about what is placed within the Realm of Control. Provide consolidation for the activity by asking the team to consider the concerns that were placed within the Realm of Control.

> *Possible Prompts:* Take a few minutes to consider the concerns that were placed within the Realm of Control. What differences do you notice between the two outer circles? What do you see? What is significant? What does it mean for our team's work?

Your team should now have a well-framed problem for their inquiry.

Note: This activity was adapted from the National School Reform Faculty. http://www.nsrfharmony.org/protocol/a_z.html#O

DETERMINING A MEANINGFUL FOCUS—CHECKING CRITERIA

As stated earlier, the most effective collaborative inquiry teams keep in mind that their end goal is to increase learning and achieve greater success for *all* students.

Ask the team to check the identified priority against the criteria. How did they do?

Is the collaborative inquiry team's focus on the following?

- Based on identified, current student learning needs
- Connected to a shared vision
- Addressing an issue individuals can act on
- Manageable for the team

DEVELOPING AN INQUIRY QUESTION

The question collaborative inquiry teams formulate will guide their professional learning and help them determine the actions required and evidence needed to make decisions throughout the process. Because of the cyclical nature of this process, teams will revisit and refine their initial questions. Early questions tend to identify actions that are too broad in nature, and often members of the team do not share a common definition of vocabulary used. For example, consider the following question: What is the impact of *differentiated instruction* on *student engagement?* As a number of learning strategies are embedded in the numerous ways to differentiate instruction, the term is too broad to include in an inquiry question. In addition, *student engagement* is an ambiguous term and facilitators will find there is little consensus among team members about how to define and measure it.

Another common error teams make when initially developing their inquiry questions is that they focus on more than one classroom practice and/or student learning outcome. Consider the following examples: What is the impact of integrating iPod technology and using a problem-solving approach on students' ability to articulate their thinking in mathematics? What is the impact of co-constructing success criteria on students' ability to set goals and provide feedback to peers? To ensure manageability, questions should identify *one* classroom practice and *one* student learning outcome.

Facilitators assist teams in developing an inquiry question that meets the following criteria:

Collaborative inquiry questions must do the following:

- Contain neutral exploratory language
- Begin with the words "how" or "what"
- Specify one adult action/change in practice
- Specify one student learning outcome

The activities in this section are designed to help facilitators lead teams in developing inquiry questions that meet these criteria.

The Purpose Statement

At this point, it is helpful to ask teams to write a purpose statement. Teams have collaborated in framing a problem by identifying a student learning need. Outlining a clear and compelling purpose for the collaborative effort will further inspire and motivate the team. Through the process of collaborative inquiry, new understandings and solutions to address problems associated with student learning are jointly constructed. Stating the purpose for the inquiry will help drive the

> "The purpose statement describes succinctly the overall intent of the inquiry" (Creswell, 2002, p. 126).

team forward in their quest to uncover solutions that will better meet the needs of the students they serve. In other words, the purpose statement gets to the core of what it is teams are trying to accomplish and make better. In addition, the purpose statement sets the direction for data collection and reporting (Stages 2 and 4).

Activity 5—Writing a Purpose Statement

Materials Needed: Paper, Pens, Examples of Purpose Statements (Resource C)

Since the purpose statement sets the direction for data collection and reporting, it is important to use language that is exploratory in nature. When teams are new to this process, they often hold the misconception that the primary purpose of collaborative inquiry is research. Therefore, they default to using quantitative methods, select pretest and posttest designs, focus on language that tries to *explain* or *predict* how one variable influences another, and often identify test scores as *the* measure to determine effectiveness. While teams have the option of choosing a quantitative approach, as the collection and analysis of numerical data can provide much insight into problems of practice, a skilled facilitator will assist teams in articulating purpose statements that use exploratory language. By doing so, the team's data collection will be directed toward a variety of sources including day-to-day observations, conversations, and student work products.

Collaborative inquiry should be viewed primarily as a professional learning strategy as opposed to a research design. It is a powerful strategy for professional learning because throughout the process, team members engage in critical reflection to make sense of their actions and assess the effects of their work. Reflection is an important component of the professional practices of educators as it facilitates their ability to learn from their experiences by examining the consequences of their actions. Engaging teams in frequently examining more immediate and complete bodies of evidence including day-to-day observations, conversations, and student work products will help team members in considering the dichotomy between their intentions and the outcomes achieved. Argyris (1999)

An additional reason to encourage teams to consider a qualitative approach is that quantitative methods are often associated with experimental designs. Team members will experience difficulty trying to operationalize variables and attempting to uncover cause-and-effect relationships. This gold standard of research is not possible in education.

referred to this as double-loop learning and noted that double-loop learning was needed when organizations were faced with complex issues.

Figure 2.3 Examples of Purpose Statements

Student Learning Need—In math, students experience difficulty applying strategies for solving problems.

Problem Framed—Students are able to perform procedures but lack conceptual understanding needed to apply learning to new and different situations when solving problems.

Purpose Statement—The purpose of this inquiry is to understand how to develop Grade 7 students' conceptual understanding of measurement.

Student Learning Need—Students lack the ability to transfer their learning by applying strategies in different contexts.

Problem Framed—Students don't automatically use visual representations (e.g., charts and graphs) to communicate their understanding in subjects other than mathematics.

Purpose Statement—The purpose of this inquiry is to explore how to assist students in the intermediate division in transferring strategies across content areas.

Providing Models. Facilitators share the Examples of Purpose Statements (Resource C) with team members. Note that each purpose statement was developed based on a problem rooted in an identified student learning need. Provide time for members to read each example and then ask the team to assess each purpose statement based on the following criteria:

Effectively developed purpose statements do the following:

- State the issue to be explored
- Use words that convey intent about the exploration of the issue such as "discover," "understand," "explore," or "describe"
- Mention the participants in the inquiry

Artifact: Facilitators might ask teams to include their purpose statement in their final report.

Writing the Statement. Provide the following formula for writing a purpose statement:

The purpose of this inquiry is to (explore? discover? describe? understand?) (the issue) for (participants). Guide your team in using the formula to write a purpose statement. The formula suggested for developing a purpose statement lends itself to a qualitative design.

Activity 6—Developing an Inquiry Question

Materials Needed: Inquiry Questions—Examples—Strong and Weak (Resource D)

As mentioned earlier, the inquiry question must meet certain criteria: When formulating the question, teams must do the following:

- Use neutral exploratory language
- Begin with the words "how" or "what"
- Specify one adult action/change in practice
- Specify one student learning outcome

In preparation, photocopy and cut out the examples of strong and weak questions (Resource D). Share the criteria for formulating an inquiry question with your team. Ask the team (in groups of two or three) to determine which questions are strong and which are weak by sorting them into categories.

Figure 2.4 Examples of Strong and Weak Inquiry Questions

1. How can we implement more effective note-taking strategies to support students in understanding and retaining information?

2. Does a sense of belonging affect academic achievement?

3. Will the use of metacognitive strategies increase students' ability to self-regulate?

4. What impact does allowing students multiple opportunities to demonstrate what they know and can do have on student learning?

5. What impact does the use of exit cards have on students' ability to identify essential understandings in a lesson/unit?

Possible Prompts: The examples on the strips of paper illustrate both strong and weak inquiry questions. Remember that well-developed questions use neutral exploratory language, begin with the words "how" or "what," and specify the focus for the team's inquiry (both the adult action and the student-learning outcomes). Read each question and sort it according to the categories "strong" and "weak."

After this activity, if teams need to deepen their understanding of what makes a strong inquiry question, facilitators might consider asking the team to revise the examples of weaker questions. How could the weaker questions be reworded to make them stronger and better reflective of the criteria? The facilitator should allow the team time to develop the inquiry question.

DEVELOPING AN INQUIRY QUESTION—CHECKING CRITERIA

Facilitators guide teams in checking their question against the criteria. How did they do?

Does the inquiry question the meet the following criteria?

- Contain neutral exploratory language
- Begin with the words "how" or "what"
- Specify one adult action/change in practice
- Specify one student-learning outcome

Finally, teams should ask themselves, "Is this a burning question? Is this something we really need to figure out?" If the answer is yes to both questions, then teams have developed a question that is worth investigating.

Once questions are formulated, they will continue to be refined. As teams cycle through the stages of collaborative inquiry, implementing changes in classroom practice and gathering and reflecting on evidence, it is common for teams to revisit and fine-tune their initial question. Teams will find themselves revisiting earlier stages as they rethink, interpret, and co-construct new understandings. Fullan (2011) suggested that educators learn while doing, noting that finding and learning from practice is what works in solving difficult problems and that developing questions accelerates and deepens the process.

FORMULATING A THEORY OF ACTION

More than thirty years ago, Argyris and Schon (1974) made significant contributions to our understanding of organizational learning, coining the phrase "theory of action" to describe people's ideas about how to accomplish tasks and goals. These theories significantly influence how individuals and groups solve problems and make choices. Bushe (2010) noted that whether people are aware of their theories, they exist and that every goal-oriented action people take is based on some theory they hold about how those actions will lead to the attainment of their goals. Theories of action come in two types: espoused theories (stated as beliefs and values) and theories-in-use (actual behavior). This distinction allows us to reflect on the incongruence between the two. Is what we say we believe emulated in our behavior?

In a study investigating the extent to which teachers' beliefs were manifested in practice, Lee (2009) provided examples that demonstrate what people often do is different from the theories they espouse, uncovering the following ten areas of discrepancy related to feedback:

> "A theory of action can be thought of as a story line that makes a vision and a strategy concrete. It gives the leader a line of narrative that leads people through the daily complexity and distractions that compete with the main work of the instructional core. It provides the map that carries the vision through the organization. And it provides a way of testing the assumptions and suppositions of the vision against the unfolding realities of the work in an actual organization with actual people." (City, Elmore, Fiarman, & Teitel, 2009, p. 40)

1. Teachers believed that good writing was more than simply form, but they provided most of their feedback in this category.

2. Teachers believed that it was best to focus feedback on specific errors or feedback for a specific purpose, but they marked errors comprehensively.

3. Teachers believed that students would benefit from locating and correcting their own errors, but they consistently corrected and located errors for students.

4. Teachers believed that students had limited ability to decipher editing codes, but they used them anyway.

5. Teachers believed that scores or grades caused students to ignore teacher feedback, but they used them anyway.

6. Teachers believed it was important to highlight students' strengths and weaknesses, but they focused usually on the weaknesses.

7. Teachers believed that students should take more responsibility for their learning, but their practices took this control away from students, making it nearly impossible.

8. Teachers believed that the writing process was helpful, but teachers asked students to write single drafts and provided feedback on these, responding to the product at the end instead of providing feedback throughout the process.

9. Teachers believed that students would continue to make the errors that the teacher corrected in their work, but teachers continued to focus on correcting student errors.

10. Teachers believed that the effort they invested in providing students with feedback was ineffective, but they did not alter their feedback practices.

Examining, reflecting on, and openly discussing the incongruence between espoused theories and theories-in-use are at the core of organizational learning. If we are going to produce meaningful changes in education, we need to recognize and acknowledge the discrepancy between what we say we believe and what we actually do. This can be difficult and challenging work as people feel a need to preserve relationships and, therefore, avoid engaging in conversations involving issues that seem too controversial to discuss. Argyris (1999) used the term "organizational defense routines" to refer to the "actions or policies intended to prevent players from experiencing embarrassment or threat in ways that make it difficult to identify and reduce the causes of the embarrassment or threat" (p. 56) arguing that counterproductive consequences (e.g., defensiveness, misunderstanding, distrust) for authentic problem-solving occur when evaluations of our own and each other's actions are surfaced. Defensiveness is a natural reaction employed to avoid threats and embarrassments associated with these dilemmas, especially if people feel the need to justify past actions. Dialogue becomes cautious, people advocate protecting the status quo, and critical issues that need to be addressed are bypassed or covered up. As a result, theories-in-use are reinforced and genuine learning is inhibited.

The collaborative inquiry process helps reduce the conditions that limit learning in organizations. Teams adopt a *learning stance* when formulating inquiries into identified problems of practice. Theiopoulou (Organization Unbound, n.d.) explained,

> Someone, in order to learn, needs to create questions and to inquire. Unless inquiry is expressed, there is no learning stance; it is instead a knowing stance, which is exactly the opposite. A knowing stance is expressed by advocating and that does not provide any opening for new information to come in, to reach our brain and as a consequence of course, to process new learning and generate new knowledge. (para. 6)

When formulating inquiries, articulating theories of action, and testing theories-in-use, individuals must abandon a *knowing stance* and adopt a *learning stance.* This is one of the reasons collaborative inquiry is considered a powerful design for professional learning.

During this first stage in the process, collaborative inquiry teams make their theories of action explicit. This involves articulating simplified causal statements that prescribe how to achieve intended consequences. Theories of action will serve two purposes. First, it will serve as a story line that will connect the team's vision with specific strategies used to improve teaching and learning (City et al., 2009). Bushe (2010) suggested that when teams are trying to accomplish a goal together, it is helpful to operate from a common theory of action. Second, it will help teams align their intended theory with the enacted theory through reflection and dialogue. Heifetz, Grashow, and Linsky (2009) noted that closing the gap between espoused theories and theories-in-use is a difficult adaptive challenge but that "individuals and organizations alike come face-to-face with their real priorities" (p. 79) when this gap can no longer be ignored.

Activity 7—Formulating a Theory of Action

> Materials Needed: Paper, Pens, Theory of Action Example (Page 30), Theory of Action T-Chart (Resource E)

The purpose of this activity is to formulate causal connections in the form of "if-then" statements. Heath and Heath (2010) noted that ideas need to be translated into specific behaviors to remove the ambiguity from a team's vision of change. Your team's theory of action will do this and be helpful in creating your data collection plan (Stage 2 of the collaborative inquiry process).

Figure 2.5 Theory of Action T-Chart

Theory of Action	
If . . . (Action)	**Then . . . (Outcome)**

Theories of action must meet the following criteria:

- Be committed to in writing
- Contain statements of causal relationships that can be disproved
- Adhere to the conditions under which continuous improvement will happen
- Include new capacities that must be developed to ensure success

City et al. (2009) suggested that committing to a theory of action in written form "provides the opportunity to test our presuppositions about what we think will work against the evidence of what actually works" (p. 56). Articulating simplified causal statements that prescribe how to achieve intended consequences will help the team in considering the causes (classroom practices) that precede the effects (student learning). Reeves (2010) noted that simplistic as it is, "in an environment where only effects matter, causes are dismissed as irrelevant" (p. 16). Theories of action can be used by facilitators to ensure that causes are not treated as immaterial. Although they are committed to in writing, Fullan (2008) reminded us of the need to remain fluid in our thinking when formulating and reformulating theories and suggested that leaders use theories to guide their actions but remain open to "new data that may direct future action" (p. 8). Fullan (2006) also noted that if theories of action do not address the conditions under which continuous improvement will happen, they are bound to fail. Finally, theories of action that include the development of individual and collective knowledge and competencies are more likely to achieve results (Fullan, 2006).

THEORY OF ACTION EXAMPLE

The following theory of action is provided as an example.

A group of secondary school department heads, from a variety of disciplines, have come together to participate in a professional learning community. The team decided to use collaborative inquiry as a process to guide their learning and work. When identifying current student learning needs, they noted that many students relied on listening alone to learn the required information and concluded that students experienced difficulty reading content-area textbooks. Many of their students seemed limited in their ability to master the informational texts that are characteristic in each of their courses. As the team progressed through Stage 1 of collaborative inquiry, they formed the following conclusions:

Student Learning Need: Students have difficulty comprehending informational texts.

Problem Framed: The specialized vocabulary and advanced text structures contained in textbooks present challenges for students.

Purpose Statement: The purpose of this inquiry is to determine how to build students' proficiency in reading and comprehending informational texts.

Inquiry Question: What is the impact of explicitly teaching text structures on students' ability to read and comprehend informational texts?

Theory of Action

> *If* we engage in collaborative inquiry focusing on strategies for teaching text structures, *then* we will be able to improve students' comprehension of informational texts across content areas.

> *If* we identify and implement common strategies to improve reading comprehension, *then* students will know what to expect when they move from class to class.

> *If* we focus on explicitly teaching text structures, *then* students will organize their thinking in a manner that will assist them in constructing meaning.

> *If* we teach students how texts are organized, *then* students will be able to read with better efficiency by selecting specific comprehension strategies that fit a particular text.

> *If* students are provided with effective strategies to help them understand what they read, *then* students will be motivated to use texts to advance their knowledge and understanding.

> *If* we meet regularly to share our learning, *then* we will be more likely to be open and transparent about the challenges we are facing.

> *If* instructional coaches assist in the classroom, *then* we will feel supported and will be more likely to try to test strategies.

Once the team has had an opportunity to review the example, ask them to use the Theory of Action T-Chart (Resource E) to formulate their theory of action.

> *Possible Prompts:* When considering your team's preferred future/destination, what are five or six things that could be done to make it happen? What might be the outcome for each action described?

Once the theory of action has been developed, facilitators ask the team to consider the following:

- Are all key stakeholders represented in the theory of action?
- Are the actions key stakeholders need to take clearly articulated?
- What are the individual and collective capacities included in the theory that need developing?
- Did the team consider how culture might be influenced with a focus on motivating people to put in the effort?
- Is the result an increase in student learning?

Ask the team to revise the theory accordingly based on the discussion.

After articulating causal statements, teams identify assumptions that are implicit in their theories of action. Then, they use practice to discover if strategies work by testing their claims and assumptions. Fullan (2011) referred to this as "deliberate doing" (p. 5) and noted it as the core learning method for effective leaders.

Activity 8—Identifying Underlying Assumptions

> Materials Needed: Theory of Action (developed by the team)

> "The world has become too complex for any theory to have certainty." (Fullan, 2008, p. 5)

The most important component of a theory of action is identifying the underlying assumptions on which the theory is based. Senge et al. (2004) note, "Breakthroughs come when people learn how to take the time to stop and examine their assumptions" (p. 33). If we do not identify the assumptions that underlie our theories and test them against real events, we run the risk of holding invalid theories and enacting behaviors that are ineffective.

The following assumptions are implicit in the secondary school department head's theory of action (depicted previously).

The team's theory of action assumes the following:

- Full participation across content areas.
- Consistency can be achieved across content areas.
- Teachers know text structures as well as strategies for teaching text structures to students.
- Teachers will be explicit in their teaching of text structures.
- Students will select appropriate strategies depending on text structures.
- Success will motivate students.

- Teachers are willing to take a learning stance and willing to work with an instructional coach.
- Success builds with an increase in practice and support.

Ask your team to revisit their theory of action to identify assumptions.

Possible Prompts: Based on the statements in the team's theory of action, what do we assume to be true? What are we taking for granted? How have these assumptions influenced our thinking about the problem framed?

FORMULATING A THEORY OF ACTION—CHECKING CRITERIA

Have your team check their theory of action against the criteria. How did they do?

- Is your team's theory of action committed to in writing?
- Does your team's theory of action contain statements of causal relationships that can be disproved?
- Does your team's theory of action adhere to the conditions under which continuous improvement will happen?
- Does your team's theory of action include new capacities that must be developed to ensure success?

At the end of Stage 1, collaborative inquiry teams will have determined a meaningful focus, developed an inquiry question, and formulated a theory of action. Teams are likely to reframe the problem, revise the question, and reformulate a theory as they proceed through the process. This is the cyclical nature of collaborative inquiry.

Fullan (2006) noted, "Nothing will count unless people develop new capacities" (p. 9) along with persistence and flexibility in "staying the course" (p. 11). As teams put actions in place and implement changes in classroom practices, they will need to develop individual and collective knowledge and competencies. In addition, resolve will be required as team members rise to meet adaptive challenges. Skilled facilitators ensure that supports are in place to build capacity and develop resolve as the team progresses through the stages of collaborative inquiry.

Artifact: You might ask teams to include their theory of action as part of their final documentation.

"Through deliberate practice, your task is to deepen your knowledge about what works and about how to support and develop others, including the particular others with whom you are working." (Fullan, 2011, p. 22)

REFLECTION FOR FACILITATORS

Reflecting on facilitation skills and approaches will help facilitators become more conscious of the differences between facilitating and leading. This will help hone facilitative skills, ultimately leading to the creation of more effective and efficient teams. Facilitators are encouraged to consider their practice and determine where they fall along the continuum regarding each item identified in the following chart. As facilitators guide teams through Stage 2 (collecting evidence), they might use this information to help them focus on the skills or approaches they wish to further develop by remaining cognizant of areas for improvement.

Table 2.1   Reflection for Facilitators

Facilitator Skills and Approaches	Level 1	Level 2	Level 3	Level 4
Builds in norm of discomfort within a safe environment	Beginning	Developing	Applying	Innovating
Ensures all voices are heard	Beginning	Developing	Applying	Innovating
Regularly builds in habit of reflection	Beginning	Developing	Applying	Innovating
Keeps equity and student achievement at the forefront	Beginning	Developing	Applying	Innovating
Seeks public commitment for action when appropriate	Beginning	Developing	Applying	Innovating

Source: Adapted from National School Reform Faculty: New York: Facilitation Standards.

ENDNOTE

1. Affinity mapping exercise source: National School Reform Faculty (NSRF). Created by Ross Peterson-Veatch. http://www.nsrfharmony.org. Reproduced with permission.

Stage 2

Collecting Evidence

Remember, we learn to do the work by doing the work.

(City, Elmore, Fiarman, &
Teitel, 2009, p. 78)

At this point, the team has identified actions they believe will assist them in making their desired outcome a reality. They have also uncovered the underlying assumptions implicit in their theories of action. Later in the process, facilitators will guide teams in checking their assumptions and revising theories accordingly.

In addition to developing knowledge and competencies, during Stage 2 of the collaborative inquiry process, teams implement changes in practice, identify sources of information that will help answer their inquiry question, and collect evidence about how their actions are impacting students. Contained in this chapter are scaffolded activities facilitators can use to guide participants through each of these processes.

DEVELOPING KNOWLEDGE, COMPETENCIES, AND SHARED UNDERSTANDINGS

Essential to the team's success is the development of individual and collective knowledge and competencies. The development of individual and collective knowledge is inherent in the process as the design is rooted in constructivist theory. Participants generate knowledge and meaning as they move through the stages, co-constructing new understandings through *learning by doing*, and reflecting on the incongruence between espoused theories and theories-in-use. Intentionality is required on the

> "What we need is a profession that constantly and collectively builds its knowledge base and corresponding expertise, where practices and their impact are transparently tested, developed, circulated, and adapted." (Hargreaves & Fullan, 2012, p. 54)

part of the facilitator to foster the development of individual and collective competencies. Bennett (2011) suggested, "If we do not first assess our own instructional repertoire, then whatever decision we make about students will be somewhat naïve" (p. 12).

As part of their inquiry question, teams have identified actions they believe, if implemented, will help to make their desired outcome a reality. Consider the following examples:

- Teaching for conceptual understanding
- Teaching for the generalization of strategies
- Teaching explicitly
- Facilitation of productive group work
- Teaching strategies for summarizing
- Teaching strategies for inferring
- Teaching skills of argumentation
- Using assessment *as* learning strategies
- Providing effective feedback
- Establishing relevance and purpose

Teams now need to a) examine their professional practices and identify strengths and gaps in their knowledge and competencies, b) learn more about and come to a common understanding about the particular practice they have identified, and c) design their instruction accordingly. Facilitators can support the team's learning and foster implementation in a variety of ways. Designing professional learning that is focused on identified student learning needs is where facilitators begin. Hirsh and Killion (2007) noted, "Students will benefit when student learning needs are the focus for educators' professional learning and the entire educational system aligns to support both students and educators" (p. 67). Facilitators can also lead teams in developing a common understanding of practice and designing instruction by using Innovation Configuration Maps (IC Maps) and Checklists. These tools are described in further detail in the section that follows.

Having a clear understanding of new practices is important if they are going to be applied effectively. Holding a common understanding of the practices will improve the consistency in which they are implemented across classrooms and enable the team to more accurately assess the impact of their actions. Hall and Hord (2006) noted that widespread change often occurs only modestly across schools because implementers and change facilitators "do not fully understand what the change is or what it will look like when it is implemented in the envisioned way" (p. 111). Gersten, Vaughn, Deshler, and Schiller (1997) noted, "When teachers receive only vague guidelines, without concrete examples and procedures, implementation of new practice is often erratic" (p. 469). Heath and Heath (2010) also reminded us that we cannot assume that new moves are obvious and that when you want someone to behave in a new way, you must "explain the new way clearly" (p. 60). Facilitators can help to remove ambiguity about new practices by engaging the team in building IC Maps or Checklists.

Activity 9—Developing an Innovation Configuration Map

Materials Needed: Innovation Configuration Map for a Cooperative Learning Initiative (Table 3.1), Innovation Configuration Map Template (Resource F)

Innovation Configuration Maps (IC Maps) are written guidelines that describe specific behaviors, spelling out what practices will look like when they are fully implemented in classrooms. IC Maps were first developed by the University of Texas Research and Development as a tool to measure school change and to assist teachers through different stages of implementation by providing descriptions of observable variations of key components of teaching practices.

The process of creating IC Maps is both interactive and iterative. Collaborative inquiry teams benefit from co-constructing IC Maps because through discussion and debate, they clarify their understandings and develop consensus about what the practice should look like when it is in use. It is a tool that individuals can use for self-reflection and goal setting. IC Maps can also be used, if mutually agreed on, as a tool during peer observation or to guide post-observation conversations. In addition, an IC Map can be used by facilitators to document the quality of implementation.

Consider the following example:

Table 3.1 Completed Innovation Configuration Map for a Cooperative Learning Initiative

Component 1: Structured Groups – The teacher...				
1	2	3	4	5
assigns students to four-member groups.	assigns students to groups larger than four.	assigns students to work with only one partner.	does not assign students to groups.	

(Continued)

Table 3.1 (Continued)

Component 2: Structured Tasks — The teacher				
1	2	3	4	5
explicitly defines tasks, learning targets, and success criteria as all group members complete the assignment.	explicitly defines tasks, learning targets, and success criteria as most group members complete the assignment.	explicitly defines tasks, learning targets, and success criteria as some group members complete the task.	specifies no learning target or success criteria.	specifies no task.

Component 3: Assures Individual Accountability — The teacher			
1	2	3	4
selects any or all group members to answer for the group and/ or gives individual tests to each student.	repeatedly selects those who typically answer correctly.	fails to solicit answers from ethnic/minority students or girls.	permits one student to complete the task and answer for the group.

Component 4: Develops Group Skills — The teacher			
1	2	3	4
explicitly states, monitors, and rewards group or social skills expected during the task.	states and monitors group skills expected to be exhibited.	states but does not monitor or reward expected group skills.	does not state, monitor, or reward group or social skills.

Component 5: Promotes Positive Interdependence — The teacher . . .			
1	2	3	4
consistently arranges tasks so that group members must depend on one another to complete it.	frequently arranges tasks so that group members must depend on one another to complete it.	occasionally arranges tasks so that group members must depend on one another to complete it.	arranges tasks that permit group members to complete it alone.

Component 6: Assesses Group Processing – The teacher . . .				
1	2	3	4	5
provides students the time and procedures to analyze how well their groups are functioning and how well they are using the necessary social skills.	continues to enhance analysis and assessment skills.	monitors the students' development of group processing analysis and assessment.	allows students to analyze and assess how their groups function.	does not give attention to analysis and assessment of group processing.

- - - - - - - - - - - - -   variations to the right are unacceptable; variations to the left are acceptable.

————————————   variations to the left are ideal.

Source: Richardson, J. (2004). Taking measure: Innovation Configurations gauge the progress of a new initiative. *Tools for Schools*. National Staff Development Council, Oxford, OH. Reprinted with permission.

In the previous example, the key elements of cooperative learning are itemized. For each key element, variations of identifiable behaviors are described, with the ideal behaviors located on the far left and the most unacceptable behaviors located on the far right. Action verbs are used to begin each sentence so that the behaviors described are both doable and observable. Fidelity lines draw a distinction between ideal, acceptable, and unacceptable behaviors. Unlike a rubric, key elements might have a different number of variations. Some key elements might have three variations while another may have five. In addition, the left to right con-figuration places the ideal variation in the most significant location for teachers.

The first step in developing an IC Map is to determine the key ele-ments of the new practice. If collaborative inquiry teams were developing an IC Map for effective feedback, for example, they might identify the key elements as purpose, focus, amount, specificity, and timing. Within each key element, teams then visualize and brainstorm the ideal behavior of individuals (e.g., principals, teachers, students). For example, if the key element is amount, an ideal might be the following:

> ## Effective Feedback: Amount
>
> The teacher *identifies* two or three main points that are related to the learning targets and outlined in the success criteria. The teacher begins by *sharing* strengths followed by *commenting* on areas for growth.

Next, teams describe unacceptable behavior.

> The teacher *identifies* every error in a student's work product, *asks* the student to correct all of the errors, and *does not provide* an opportunity for the student to resubmit the assignment (or an alternative) for reevaluation.

The team then brainstorms variations of each key element, filling in the gaps between the ideal and the unacceptable behaviors. Facilitators should ensure that action verbs are used to describe the behavior of individuals as the team records the key elements and behaviors in a chart. The final step entails the team determining the lines of fidelity that will discriminate acceptable behaviors from unacceptable behaviors.

Activity 10—Developing a Checklist

Another way facilitators assist team members in developing competencies and shared understandings of new practices is to engage them in developing a checklist. Gawande (2009) suggested that a checklist could be used as "a simple tool for people to try in hopes of improving their results" (p. 151) and that they could help the group in finding a way to ensure that they let "nothing fall between the cracks" (p. 103). Checklists set out the minimum necessary steps in a process and make them clear, establishing "a higher standard of baseline performance" (p. 39). Developing a checklist that outlines the critical elements of the action will help ensure the nuances of the practice are well understood by each team member.

Consider the following example:

Gawande (2009) suggested that checklists should not be lengthy and that developers should only include five to nine items (the limit of working memory) on the list. Developing a checklist will assist collaborative inquiry teams in identifying the critical attributes necessary for ensuring the fidelity of the new practice being implemented. In addition, the checklist could be used by team members as a tool to provide objective feedback during peer observations.

> ## Explicit Instruction Checklist
>
> ☐ Review previous learning (activate prior knowledge)
> ☐ Identify learning targets (from Common Core State Standards in student-friendly language)
> ☐ Model or demonstrate procedures (show how something is done—think aloud and explain the processes used)
> ☐ Provide examples and nonexamples (using visual prompts if possible)
> ☐ Engage students in doing (using a variety of methods including cooperative learning)
> ☐ Check for understanding (use the information to adjust instruction)

There are many other ways facilitators can foster the development of knowledge and competencies and common understandings of practices. Selecting and sharing relevant reading material is one way to help inform practice related to the team's inquiry. In addition, as the team implements new practices, facilitators can encourage team members to engage in peer observation. Reeves (2008) suggested, "The direct observation of the professional practices of teachers by teachers must become the new foundation of professional development" (p. 3). Whatever the approach, it is important that facilitators provide support for professional learning by structuring opportunities in which teams gain a deeper understanding of sound instructional practices related to their inquiry for improving student learning.

IMPLEMENTING CHANGES IN PRACTICE

Newly acquired understandings of effective instruction must be enacted if teams hope to impact student learning. To achieve implementation success, facilitators should keep the following suggestions in mind.

1. Keep the changes small and few.

If teachers are required to make considerable changes in their practices, it is unlikely that they will adopt new approaches. Gersten et al. (1997) noted that innovations that do not ask teachers to radically change what they do are more likely to be adopted and offered an example of a study in which teachers asked students to generate predictions and then assess their accuracy. The authors indicated, "For many teachers it was a first step toward teaching reading in a more constructivist fashion" (p. 470). However, observations revealed that teachers "would ask students to generate predictions but would not follow up by asking the class to evaluate whether the predictions were supported by the text" (p. 470). The authors believed that the overall low quality of this practice was in part due to the scale in which it was implemented and the failure to provide sustained professional development.

Heath and Heath (2010) suggested that change facilitators not only need to *script the critical moves* (as accomplished through an IC Map or Checklist) but that they must also *shrink the change* noting that if a task feels too large, people will resist. Facilitators might consider *shrinking the change* by identifying learning progressions and introducing key elements in small increments. This will assist in ensuring that the scope and magnitude of the identified change remains manageable for team members.

Consider the following example. A collaborative inquiry team has identified the implementation of a three-part lesson plan as a strategy that they believe will assist students in retaining information and transferring problem-solving skills in mathematics. In the three-part lesson, the purpose of part one is to prime students for learning by establishing a positive learning environment, activating prior learning, and engaging their affective and cognitive domains. The second part focuses on the processing of information through the provision of time for practice and application using a gradual release of responsibility framework. In the final part, teachers provide opportunities for consolidation and reflection while checking for conceptual understanding. Rather than asking teachers to consider and implement strategies that address all three parts at the onset, facilitators might ask the team to develop one part of the lesson only. Once teachers have mastered one part, facilitators could help team members identify appropriate next steps.

2. Stay with it long enough to get good at it and strive for deep implementation.

As cognitive science continues to provide new insights into how people learn, staff developers are constantly reintroducing proven practices in school systems, focusing efforts on one approach and then another. Instead of being viewed as a reinforcement of existing practices, with slight revisions or modifications based on new understandings, some educators misconstrue them as something new altogether. Alternatively, some educators view approaches as "repacked" initiatives that were initially misunderstood, poorly implemented, and whose viability was dismissed for various reasons. Unfortunately, in both cases, resistance often results when educators are asked repeatedly to adopt what they perceive as a new or ineffective approach. School districts do not stay with change initiatives long enough to enable staff to fully understand the approach or to buy into the change.

Hall and Hord (2006) suggested that institutions typically invest heavily in the development of innovations in terms of people, time, and resources, while failing to "acknowledge that implementation requires an equal investment of time and money" (p. 6). Hirsh and Killion (2007) also placed the blame on the imbalance of resources devoted to planning as opposed to implementation as a plausible explanation for why districts experience limited results. Reeves (2008) noted that most projects are declared failures because efforts are abandoned well before deep teacher engagement happens and provided evidence that only at deep levels of implementation (efforts in which 90% or more of the staff implemented a strategy) do efforts significantly improve student achievement. Many school districts do not provide enough implementation support to reach impact at a student achievement level and abandon efforts well before results can be realized.

Unfortunately, a similar phenomenon takes place as teachers implement changes in their classrooms. Often, teachers do not stay with strategies long enough to impact student learning. Guskey (2000) stated, "New practices are likely to be abandoned in the absence of any evidence of their positive effects" (p. 141). The dichotomy is that when individuals first try something new, their skill level is not very high and it is unlikely that they will see any evidence of positive effects. Marzano's (2011) research provided evidence to support this notion. The author pointed out that differences in reported effects on student learning of various instructional strategies can be explained by examining four levels of implementation. When teachers are at the first level of use (beginning level), the strategy probably has little effect on student learning. As teachers progress with implementation, they become more effective in using the strategy. When teachers are at the fourth level of implementation (innovating level), they have become so familiar with the strategy that they can adapt it to meet specific student needs. Hall and Hord (2006) also pointed out that as people implement new practices, they shift through progressive levels of skills. Initially, because people are trying to master the tasks required, it results in disjointed and superficial use. Because they do not see immediate impact of their actions, teachers abandon strategies before they reach an innovating level of implementation.

Reeves (2009) noted, "We can develop leaders whose focus and vision prevent them from believing that plans are a substitute for action. We can nurture leaders who understand that deep implementation, not a timid incremental approach, is essential for systemic change" (p. 55).

Facilitators of collaborative inquiry teams need to ensure teams stay the course while striving for deep levels of implementation.

3. Ensure supportive conditions are in place onsite.

Fullan, Hill, and Crévola (2006) identified professional learning that was both school-based and embedded in teachers' daily work as the most effective way to change classroom instruction. For this to occur, onsite supports are needed. Hord (2008) identified structural and relational conditions as one of the five components in regard to how effective learning communities function. Defining structural conditions as a time and place to meet along with policies and resources that support staff in coming together to learn and relational conditions as positive attitudes, trust, and respect, the author noted that these must be in place to support intentional learning. Guskey (2000) also noted that organizational support must be in place for teachers to implement changes in practice.

Joyce, Showers, and Rolheiser-Bennett (1987) were first to highlight the benefits of providing onsite supports, by demonstrating the likelihood of teachers transferring new skills into practice was 90% when in-situational coaching was provided. More recently, Knight (2009) reported findings from a study in which half of the teachers who received after-school training in new teaching strategies were assigned a coach to provide follow-up support. Observers reported that the newly taught strategies were used during 90% of their observational visits in the classes taught by teachers who received coaching as opposed to a 30% transfer by teachers who did not. Increasingly, school boards are allocating a greater percentage of professional development funds to support in-situational coaching as the necessity of this type of follow-up support in promoting transfer to practice and changing classroom instruction is being more widely acknowledged.

If individuals in formal coaching roles are not available to assist in the classroom, facilitators might consider partnering team members to serve as peer coaches. Murray, Ma, and Mazur (2009) described peer coaching as a "mutual consultation between teachers of equal status" (p. 203) making the distinction from other forms of coaching where hierarchal relationships exist. Peer coaching differs from other types of coaching in that partnerships are formed between fellow teachers. Each participant acts as the coach and the coachee, providing one another with support and assistance. In this two-way relationship, pairs focus on practice and results—not on each other's competence. Peer coaching increases the likelihood that teachers will commit to a long-term application of new acquired knowledge and competencies.

4. Encourage principal's involvement and support her learning.

It is imperative that administrators gain an understanding of new practices if they are to be fully realized in classrooms. Bennett (2011) noted, "Any school staff where the principal is not involved in the instructional innovation the staff is attempting to implement is unlikely to get very far as a staff; you will get a few 'keeners' doing it, but if it were a business, you would be out of work" (p. 15). Knight (2007) stated that approaches that did "not have the principal's guiding hand as the instructional leader will lead to teachers adopting teaching practices but unsystematically—with some and not others implementing the change so school improvement may progress incoherently" (p. 27). When leaders have a clear understanding of new practices, they will be better equipped to support teachers' use of them, leading to deeper levels of implementation. One way facilitators can promote this is to invite principals to be contributing team members, engaging in the process of inquiry while learning alongside their staff.

This is the sixth principle of the instructional core outlined by City, Elmore, Fiarman, and Teitel (2009). The authors noted, "You can't create a common culture of practice without actually engaging in the practice yourself" (p. 33). The sixth principle states, "We learn to do the work by doing the work, not by telling other people to do the work, not by having done the work at some time in the past, and not by hiring experts who can act as proxies for our knowledge about how to do the work" (p. 33). A skilled facilitator will assist principals in making connections between the team's work and their leadership practice. For example, if "effective feedback" is the strategy teams are going to implement into classroom practice, facilitators can assist principals in identifying authentic opportunities in which *they* can deliver effective feedback (e.g., teacher performance appraisals). If it is a three-part lesson plan, facilitators can assist principals in modeling this format during school-based professional learning sessions.

Not only does the principal's understanding of new practices have an impact on her ability to visibly, vocally, and actively support changes in classroom instruction, but her participation in the cycle of inquiry will help her to understand the power inherent in the design. By participating in collaborative inquiry, principals will gain an appreciation of how the professional learning approach can be used to effectively address challenging issues related to school improvement. If collaborative inquiry is going to become a way of doing business in schools, principals need a deep understanding of the concepts, which can only be gained by participating in the cycle.

When principals participate in the learning, not only are levels of implementation increased but student learning is impacted as well.

Robinson, Lloyd, and Rowe (2008) conducted a metaanalysis from studies that examined the relationship between leadership and student outcomes, comparing the effects of five leadership practices on student outcomes. This metaanalysis showed that there were "substantial differences between the leadership of otherwise similar high- and low-performing schools, and that those differences matter for student academic outcomes" (p. 657). In the high-performing schools, teachers reported that leaders were a) more focused on teaching and learning, b) stronger instructional resources for teachers, and c) more active participants in and leaders of teacher learning and development. When leaders promoted and participated in teacher learning, it involved more than just supporting or sponsoring other staff in their learning. The leader was a participant in the learning as leader, learner, or both. The principal's involvement in teacher learning provided them with a "deep understanding of the conditions required to enable staff to make and sustain the changes required for improved outcomes" (p. 667). The researchers concluded, "The closer educational leaders get to the core business of teaching and learning, the more likely they are to have a positive impact on students' outcomes" (p. 664).

DEVELOPING THE DATA COLLECTION PLAN

Now that the collaborative inquiry team has described and defined the change they are going to implement in classroom practice, they can begin to consider what data to collect to answer their inquiry question and guide their instructional planning. This is a critical step in the process as the aspects of the plan have important implications for the quality of the team's findings. To support the team in developing a well-thought-out data collection plan, facilitators must ensure that the team considers certain criteria.

A well-developed plan for data collection meets the following criteria:

- Is committed to in writing
- Includes a variety of valid and reliable measures
- Outlines with transparency how the evidence will be collected
- Indicates when the evidence will be collected and by whom
- Ensures a manageable process for collection—given available time and resources

At this stage, a well-developed plan for collecting data is critical for the team's future success. Facilitators should be aware of a few common errors made when teams are new to this process. The first error is that they collect too much evidence. In the end, they are overwhelmed with the amount of data and do not have the time to analyze what they have collected. Second, they identify and collect evidence that does not measure the student learning outcome and come to this realization in Stage 3 when they collectively analyze the evidence. When this happens, individuals often feel their efforts were in vain and feel the need to rush back through the process in an effort to collect the *right* evidence. Another common error that occurs during this stage is that teams predominately identify achievement test data (and often focus on pretest and posttest designs) as the measure to answer their inquiry question. A skilled facilitator will ensure that a) the team does not overwhelm themselves by collecting too much data, b) the evidence identified is a valid measure of the student learning outcome identified, and c) the team considers a variety of evidence obtained through a variety of measures including observations, conversations, and/ or the examination of student work products. Facilitators should encourage the team to consider evidence as opposed to proof. Guskey (2006) noted that obtaining proof "requires a level of experimental rigor that is hard and often impossible to attain in practical school settings" (p. 13).

Types of Data to Consider

There are different types of data that teams could consider as well as different sources and methods of collection. Each is described in the section that follows. Bernhardt (2000) described four types of data that could be used for school improvement, which includes student learning data, demographic data, perceptual data, and school process data.

Student Learning Data. Student learning data are the assessments and evaluations teachers make about student learning based on day-to-day observations, conversations, and student work products. This information is helpful to collaborative inquiry teams when they are considering current results—how are we doing right now? Large-scale standardized assessments are also a rich source of student learning data, but these only provide trailing indicators. Bernhardt (2000) noted that student learning data tell schools which students are succeeding academically and which are not. Teams use student learning data to guide their planning, leadership, partnership, and professional development efforts in relation to their inquiries.

Demographic Data. Demographic data describe the school context showing who the students, staff, and community are and how they change over time. Some examples include enrollment, attendance, percentage of students in applied and academic streams, first language spoken at home, number of students with individual education plans, percentage of students receiving free and/or reduced lunch, teacher's qualifications, and the like. Bernhardt (2000) noted that these data provide the overarching context for everything that the school does with respect to school improvement. Collaborative inquiry teams use demographic data to help inform whether they are achieving greater success for *all* students. They may also use it to determine the allocation of resources and to pinpoint where to provide additional supports.

Perceptual Data. Perceptual data tell us about student, parent, and staff satisfaction with the work of the school (Bernhardt, 2000). Perceptual data can help the team understand how internal efforts are meeting the learning needs of students by examining feelings and opinions regarding changes in practice. Perceptual data can be gathered in a variety of ways including questionnaires and interviews from a variety of sources including students, parents, and educators.

School Process Data. Bernhardt (n.d.) described school process data as "what learning organizations, and those who work in them, are doing to help students learn: what they teach, how they teach, and how they assess students. School processes include programs, curriculum, instruction and assessment strategies, interventions, and all other classroom practices that teachers use to help students learn" (p. 1). The author noted that school process data are readily available to document. Gathering information about school processes is one way teams could monitor the degree of implementation of practices. It is also necessary to collect in order for team members to make sense of their actions and assess the effects of their work.

Of the four types of data described here, student learning data will likely be the most relevant for collaborative inquiry teams if their inquiry questions were developed based on identified student learning needs. Demographic data may also be important to collect if the team is interested in examining disparity among groups of students. The collection of school process data will be helpful in determining the extent to which the teacher action identified in the inquiry question was put into practice. Finally, teams may also find it useful to collect perceptual data, if it will help them to answer their inquiry question.

Data Sources and Methods of Collection

Within each type of data (student learning data, demographic data, perceptual data, and school process data), a range of possible data sources and methods in which to collect the data exist. As collaborative inquiry teams are identifying the types of data that will help to inform their inquiry, facilitators should encourage teams to consider a variety of sources and methods of collection. For example, sources for the category "student learning data" might include student reflections and feedback (collected using exit cards, interviews, etc.), report card grades (previously collected), and results from formal and informal classroom assessments (collected through direct observation, conversations, checklists, rating scales, paper-pencil tasks, performance tasks, and/or student portfolios, etc.). Collecting data from a variety of sources will help teams gain a more vivid picture of what is happening in connection to the problem framed. The choice of data sources depends on the inquiry question, time and resources, and the availability of individuals. As noted earlier, in addition to collecting evidence related to the student learning need, teams will also need to monitor implementation of the adult action articulated in their inquiry questions. The following activity and the Data Collection Plan Template (Resource G) have been provided to assist teams in developing a data collection plan that meets the outlined criteria.

> Keep in mind that much data already exists in schools. Some of the most frequently used and easily obtainable sources of data can make the collection process much easier. Ask participants to first consider the information that is readily available to them as opposed to information they must make an effort to collect.

> The terms "data" and "evidence" are being used interchangeably throughout this book. When people hear the word "data," they often think of numbers. By purposefully interchanging the word "data" with the word "evidence", facilitators will help teams in considering qualitative as well as quantitative sources.

Activity 11—Completing the Data Collection Plan

Materials Needed: Data Collection Plan Template (Resource G)

The purpose of this activity is to ensure that the evidence teams choose to collect will be valid, reliable, and triangulated.

Triangulation is the process of corroborating evidence from different sources (e.g., credit accumulation, student work products, report card grades, exit cards). By verifying themes from more than two sources, validity is strengthened.

What evidence is going to be collected? Distribute a copy of the Data Collection Plan Template

> "Validity refers to accuracy of interpretation and use of the data and answers the following questions: How well does the data measure what we are trying to understand? Does the interpretation of the data lead to appropriate conclusions and consequences?" (Earl & Katz, 2006, p. 57)

"Reliability addresses the following questions: How sure are we? How confident are we that these data provide enough consistent and stable information to allow us to make statements about it with certainty?" (Earl & Katz, 2006, p. 57)

(Resource G) to team members. It is important for the team to record their inquiry question in the space provided. This will assist the facilitator in steering the team in selecting evidence that is both valid and reliable by keeping the team focused on the student learning outcome identified in their question. Ask the team to complete the first column in the chart by determining three sources of evidence that will help to inform their inquiry. These three sources should be measures related to the student learning outcome identified in inquiry questions. For example, if the team's question was, "How does elimination of number grades throughout the year impact students' attitudes," three sources of evidence should be related to students' attitudes. Or if the team's question was, "How can we implement assessment *as* learning strategies in order to support students' ability to monitor their understanding," three sources of evidence should be related to students' ability to monitor their understanding. Although this seems straightforward, teams often experience difficulty matching types of data and sources to their questions.

Figure 3.1 Data Collection Plan

Inquiry Question: _____		
What evidence is going to be collected?	**How is the evidence going to be collected?**	**When is the evidence going to be collected? By whom?**
Data Source 1 (related to the student learning need identified)		
Data Source 2 (related to the student learning need identified)		

A skilled facilitator will ensure that the team selects three sources related to the student learning outcome by directing the team's attention back to the intended outcome articulated in the inquiry question. This is an important part of the process as once the data collection plan is complete, teams set off to collect the evidence identified. It will be disheartening for all if they come back to realize that they were not measuring what they thought they were measuring.

Possible Prompts: What evidence related to the student learning outcome do we already have? What evidence do we need to gather? What is the best way to determine if any changes in student learning have occurred? What will we accept as evidence? What or who is the best source of information about the intended change? Do we have three sources upon which to measure changes in intended learning outcomes?

Once the team has completed column one, for *each source* identified, ask the team to consider the following:

- Are we measuring what we *think* we are measuring?
- How much confidence do we have in this data source?

In considering all *three sources* ask the team the following:

- Are we gathering evidence from different groups/key stakeholders or is all the evidence coming from one group (e.g., students, teachers)?
- Is this evidence going to be too difficult to collect or can we do so given current resources and time?

Provide the team time to revise Column 1 based on the discussion.

How is the evidence going to be collected? There are many different ways teams can collect data. For example, teams might conduct a survey, administer a questionnaire, assign tasks to students, observe, talk to individual students about their learning, or hold focus group interviews. Teams may consider unobtrusive data collection techniques by accessing information that is already available. This information may include results from large-scale assessments, report cards, individual education plans, mark books, student portfolios, and the like. Determining which technique for collecting data will make the most sense for your team will depend on the sources identified. It is important, however, when eliciting information about student learning, that facilitators encourage the team to triangulate to include observation, student-teacher conversations, and student products. This will enable teams to verify the data they collect against one another, which will provide a more accurate portrayal of student progress.

> During this stage, it is likely that teams will revise their inquiry questions. If questions include terms that are too broad in nature, they will narrow the terms as they consider types of evidence and data sources. Also, if questions contain vague terminology, teams will refine the terms as they consider how to go about measuring student learning outcomes and monitoring adult actions.

"Teachers can gather information about learning by: tasks that provide students with a variety of ways to demonstrate their learning; observing students as they perform tasks; posing questions to help students make their thinking explicit; engineering classroom and small-group conversations that encourage students to articulate what they are thinking and further develop their thinking." (Ministry of Education, Ontario, 2010)

It is likely that teams will rely heavily on student products as a measure of the student learning outcome. As the team completes the second column in the chart, the facilitator should encourage the team to consider eliciting information about student learning through observation and conversations as well. Provide time for the team to revise their data collection plan accordingly.

When is the evidence going to be collected? By whom? The team needs to determine when and by whom the evidence will be collected. The inquiry question determines the evidence needed to make decisions and the source and methods for data collection. In addition, it is important for teams to determine a timeline as the analysis of the evidence will help inform the team's next steps. Teams that wait to gather evidence at the end of a learning period or the end of a school semester will miss valuable opportunities to use the evidence to guide instructional practice. Data collection must also be realistic to fit into the normal work patterns of a school; otherwise, the process becomes cumbersome, and eventually, it will be abandoned. It is important to remember that data collection is something we do naturally and to search for ways to build on existing and naturally occurring data collection rather than creating complicated schemes. Ask team members to complete the final column in the Data Collection Plan (When is the evidence going to be collected?). Facilitators may also encourage the team to include the name of the person(s) who will be responsible for collecting the evidence.

Evidence of Implementation of Practice

When teams cycle through this process, it is common for them to select one or two sources of the three (Column 1) that relate to the adult actions identified. The space titled "Evidence of Implementation of Practice" is provided for the team to reflect on the implementation of the adult actions that should be monitored separately. If your team developed an IC Map or a Checklist, these tools will serve as sources of evidence of implementation. Other sources that will assist the team in determining the level of implementation might be lesson plans and day books. Ask the team to consider the evidence that will help them determine the degree of implementation of the adult actions specified in their question. Teams can make a record of that information in the space provided.

DEVELOPING A DATA COLLECTION PLAN—CHECKING CRITERIA

Now your team should have a well-developed plan for collecting evidence that will be used to inform their next actions. Ask your team to check the plan against the criteria identified.

- Is the data collection plan committed to in writing?
- Does the data collection plan include a variety of valid and reliable data sources?
- Does the data collection plan outline with transparency how the evidence will be collected?
- Does the data collection plan indicate when the evidence will be collected and by whom?
- Does the data collection plan ensure a manageable process for collection—given available time and resources?

By the end of Stage 2, collaborative inquiry teams will have begun to develop individual and collective knowledge and competencies and shared understandings of new instructional practices. They will have a well-developed plan to collect evidence that is reliable, valid, and triangulated. In the process, it is likely that teams revised their inquiry question so that the adult action identified was stated with greater precision and the student learning outcome measurable. This is the cyclical nature of collaborative inquiry.

> Artifact: You might ask teams to include their plan for collecting data in their final report.

Teams must now implement new instructional practices. This might prove to be difficult and challenging work. City et al. (2009) noted, "Making meaningful and productive changes in instructional practice requires us to confront how they upset and, in some sense, reprogram our past ways of doing things" (p. 22). As noted previously, it is important to support the team through the distress and conflict that often accompany change as individuals begin to question long-held fundamental beliefs and values. Hall and Hord (2006) reminded us, "Change facilitators on the implementation side have to have a great deal of patience and persistence" (p. 7). The facilitator will need to assist the team in implementing changes in instruction, continuing to build individual and collective knowledge and competencies, reflecting on and sharing their new understandings, and maintaining timelines for data collection. In Stage 3, teams analyze data and interpret evidence so that they can determine the next course of action.

REFLECTION FOR FACILITATORS

Facilitators are once again encouraged to reflect on their practice to modify approaches and further develop facilitation skills. Table 3.2 identifies five skills and approaches of effective facilitators in addition to the items presented at the conclusion of Stage 1. Facilitators might revisit the initial five and combined with their assessment of these additional skills, determine areas in which to maintain focus during Stage 3 (analyzing evidence) for improvement.

Table 3.2   Reflection for Facilitators

Facilitator Skills and Approaches	Level 1	Level 2	Level 3	Level 4
Helps group develop the habit of making controversy public	Beginning	Developing	Applying	Innovating
Values and uses awareness of group development	Beginning	Developing	Applying	Innovating
Builds mutual accountability and is accountable to group	Beginning	Developing	Applying	Innovating
Engages group in reflection regarding values and practice	Beginning	Developing	Applying	Innovating
Adjusts time as needed	Beginning	Developing	Applying	Innovating

Source: Adapted from National School Reform Faculty: New York: Facilitation Standards.

Stage 3

Analyzing Evidence

Expert teachers are always consolidating what they know to be effective, testing it, and continuously adding to it. It's not just the evidence, but what you do with it, how you evaluate it here and now, and how you connect it to other evidence, including the evidence of your own collective experience, that matters.

(Hargreaves & Fullan, 2012, p. 54)

Although timelines for collecting evidence must remain flexible, there will be a time when teams need to come together to analyze the evidence. The data collection plans that the collaborative inquiry team developed during Stage 2 (collecting evidence) will help facilitators determine when it is time to move teams on to Stage 3 (analyzing evidence). Even though there is a certain formality in the process as it is recommended that team members analyze evidence systematically and collectively, facilitators must allow for fluidity. As teams engage in this process, they might determine that additional evidence is needed before conclusions can be drawn. What is important at this stage is that the data be examined in relation to resolving the inquiry question. Both data collection and data analysis ends when the team feels they have enough information to address the question posed.

During this stage, teams must not only consider the evidence related to the student learning need that was collected, but also the evidence related to the implementation of practice. Hall and Hord (2006) note, "A critical step in determining whether a new approach is making a difference is to determine first if the innovation is being used" (p. 159). As Marzano (2011) pointed out, levels of implementation help explain variations in the reported effects on student learning of various instructional strategies. Reeves (2008) also provided evidence that only at deep levels of implementation did efforts significantly improve student achievement. Teams should consider levels of implementation related to all other evidence gathered. If efforts were abandoned prior to deep implementation, teams need to consider how much confidence they can place in the data.

In addition, as teams examine the evidence, their beliefs may be challenged. Earl and Katz (2006) note, "Looking at data is time-consuming, but it can be fascinating. Different people will have different ideas, and conversations will be wide-ranging. Interpretation takes discipline and hard work, so the process to consider it needs to be carefully planned to give people time and support to think about and challenge their views—individually and collectively" (p. 65). During this stage, teams reflect about underlying assumptions of a specific practice and its effect on student learning. This implies that teams are evaluating their actions and beliefs. The team might revise its theory of action as new information may upset previous thoughts and ideas.

The activities in this chapter are designed to assist facilitators in supporting collaborative inquiry teams as they interpret evidence, reflect on their actions, and determine their next course of action. Collaborative inquiry teams use a five-step approach to analyzing data. The five steps include organizing, reading, describing, classifying, and interpreting. The first step involves organizing the evidence so that it can be studied. Once the data are organized, analysis begins using four iterative steps: reading, describing, classifying, and interpreting. This cyclical process is shown in Figure 4.1

Figure 4.1   Data Analysis—A Five-Step Approach

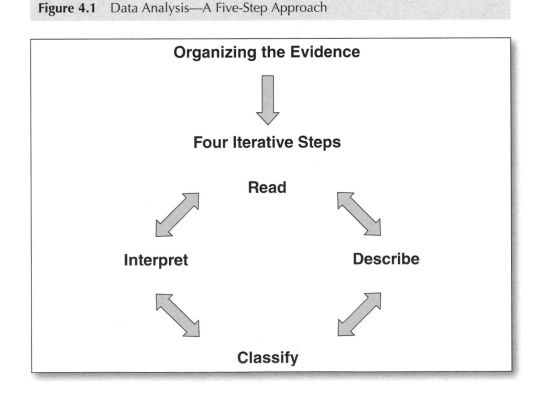

When thinking about the steps involved in analyzing data, readers are encouraged to consider the vignette woven throughout this chapter. The vignette demonstrates the stages of collaborative inquiry conducted by teachers from an intermediate division in an elementary school. Examining the stages of inquiry through another team's journey will assist facilitators in better understanding the entire process as well as the steps involved in analyzing data.

> The interrelationships among these steps are not necessarily linear. At the beginning of the analysis, the logical sequence of activities goes from reading to describing, to classifying, to interpreting. However, as the team begins to internalize and reflect on the evidence, the initial ordered sequence may lose its structure and become more flexible.

Vignette—A Professional Learning Community in Action

A group of history, science, and English teachers, with common preparation time, formed a professional learning community and agreed to engage in collaborative inquiry. As this team of six intermediate teachers from Main Street Public School progressed through the stages of collaborative inquiry, they identified the following:

> Student Learning Need: Students have a difficult time backing their opinions.
> Evidence: When asked to provide support for their answers or explain their reasoning, reasons are often weak or irrelevant and support is vague or insufficient.
> Problem Framed: Students do not know how to provide relevant reasons and sufficient support when conveying an opinion.

Every teacher agreed this was true of students in their respective disciplines. After reviewing the Common Core Standards, noting that students are required to distinguish between fact and opinion and write opinion pieces that provide logically ordered reasons supported by facts and details, the team devised the following question:

> Inquiry Question: What is the impact of visible learning strategies on students' ability to form and support opinions?

After considering a number of strategies that could be used to make thinking visible and consulting with the school's instructional coach, the team revised its question.

> Revised Inquiry Question: What is the impact of the think-aloud strategy on students' ability to share opinions with detailed and relevant reasons accompanied by clear and sufficient support?

> The revised question is less broad than the original.

The team agreed to implement the think-aloud strategy in each of their classrooms. The team developed the following theory of action.

Theory of Action

If we engage in collaborative inquiry focusing on supporting opinions across different content areas, *then* students will have a better understanding of how to effectively support an opinion.

If we use the think-aloud strategy, *then* students will hear our thought processes as we provide reasons and support for our opinions.

If we provide opportunities for students to respond to opinion prompts regularly, *then* they will get better with practice.

If we monitor the work of three "marker students" each, *then* our actions will be better informed.

If we provide opportunities for students to think aloud while pairing with another student, *then* they will further improve because of having heard their classmate's thinking.

If we meet regularly to share our learning, *then* we will be more likely to be open and transparent about the challenges we are facing.

Marker students are students teachers select for the purpose of tracking and sharing their progress over time. They are usually students who perform at or below the standard. Teachers monitor the success of the strategy for the marker students and report to their PLC.

After developing their theory of action, the team considered the skill they wanted to teach (supporting an opinion) and how they were going to teach it (think-aloud). After discussing different ways to support an opinion, the conversation turned to the strategy. Team members had different interpretations of think-aloud. One teacher thought the strategy involved asking students questions to expose thinking; another believed it entailed being explicit by stating each step needed to complete a task; another thought it involved targeting specific problems noted in student learning. The team decided to create a checklist to develop a common understanding of the strategy and to ensure consistency from one classroom to the next. Team members agreed to use this checklist when planning think-alouds for their class. With the assistance of an instructional coach, the following checklist was developed:

Think-Aloud for Supporting an Opinion Checklist

☐ Explain why you are modeling (tell students what you want them to learn)

☐ Model (put yourself in the role of the learner by thinking through the process)

- Share the question/issue in which you need to form an opinion
- State your opinion
- Show how you provide a detailed and relevant reason for your opinion
- Show how you provide support for the reason (e.g., anecdote, statistic, analogy, example)

☐ Debrief (ask students to identify processes and strategies used)

Next, in each of their subject areas, they developed an opinion prompt and planned their think-aloud scripts.

Next is an example of one of the scripts developed by an English teacher.

Sample Script: Think-Aloud for Supporting an Opinion

Have you ever had a *strong* opinion about something? Perhaps it's something you've been absolutely convinced about or something you believe with no doubt. It can be frustrating when people don't share the same opinion that you do. I'm sure there have been times when you have encountered people who have opinions that are opposed to yours—like your friends, parents, or teachers.

When sharing your opinion, especially when people hold opposing points of view, it is important to provide quality support for your opinion. There are different types of support that you can use. Knowing this will assist you in persuading people to think differently and perhaps consider *your* opinion more carefully.

Today we are learning about different ways to support an opinion. I am going to use a think-aloud to model how to support an opinion. As I do, pay careful attention to the reasons I give for my opinion, the types of support I consider, and the how I determine which type of support to provide for my reason.

> ■ Explain why you are modeling (tell students what you want them to learn)

Our school's social committee met last week and the question arose as to whether we should allow students from other schools attend the upcoming dance.

My opinion is that we should *not* allow students from other schools to attend our spring dance.

Now in thinking about my reason, to convince people, I have to ensure the reason I provide is

> ■ Model (put yourself in the role of the learner by thinking through the process)

specific and relevant. I could simply say, "They don't belong," but that is a bit vague. The reason I provide needs to be more specific so that I can provide support for it. So rather than saying, "They don't belong," I could say, "One reason is that having students from surrounding schools at the dance might encourage fighting among students, especially since we're sports rivals with them." That reason is a lot more specific.

Now I have to provide support for my reason. I wonder if any *statistics* show that admitting outsiders into dances resulted in violence. I haven't read anything like that lately or heard anything on the news and I don't have access to the Internet at this time, so I won't use a *statistic*. I wonder if I can come up with an *analogy*. Is there some sort of comparison I could make? I always get stuck trying to think of good comparisons. I am much better coming up with *examples*. Maybe I could think of a good *example*. Do I know of an *example?* Last year, I recall a group of students at Anywhere Public School began a large brawl at a fall dance. The students were from neighboring schools that didn't attend Anywhere School but were invited to the dance anyway. Several people were hurt, and the gymnasium was damaged. That's a pretty good *example*. I think I will use that *example*. Next time, I will try to think of an *analogy*.

So in answering the question, "Should we allow students from other schools to attend our spring dance?" I am going to offer the following *opinion, reason,* and *support:* We should not allow students from other schools to attend our spring dance. One *reason* is that having students from surrounding schools at the dance might encourage fighting among students, especially since we're sports rivals with them. Last October, during a dance at Anywhere Public School, students from neighboring schools began a large fight. Several kids were hurt, and there was some property damage in the gym.

■ Debrief (ask students to identify processes and strategies used)

While debriefing, the teacher planned to ask students to identify the three different ways she considered in supporting the reason for her opinion (e.g., statistic, analogy, and an example). The teacher would also ask students to consider the steps in the task while recording students' responses on a chart paper so that they would be able to refer to it for future use.

The anchor chart might read like this:

Forming and Supporting Opinions

State your opinion.

Provide a reason for your opinion (detailed and relevant).

Provide support for the reason (anecdote, statistic, analogy, example, etc.).

Finally, the teacher planned to ask students how he used knowledge of his own learning to guide his decisions. The teacher would then provide students with opportunities to practice (first in groups and pairs prior to individually) using a prompt that required students to form and support an opinion.

Once each team member had their first think-aloud script planned, the team developed the following plan for collecting data.

Table 4.1   Example of a Data Collection Plan

Data Collection Plan: Main Street Public School—Intermediate Division

Inquiry Question: What is the impact of the think-aloud strategy on students' ability to share opinions with detailed and relevant reasons accompanied by clear and sufficient support?

What evidence is going to be collected?	How is the evidence going to be collected?	When is the evidence going to be collected? By whom?
Data Source 1 *Student Learning Data* *Student written responses to opinion prompts.*	*Student Journals (used to record opinion prompts and students' responses across all participating subject areas)* *Note: Each teacher will choose three marker students to track.*	*A minimum of one prompt will be given every two weeks in each subject area (English, science, and history) during the months of October and November.*
Data Source 2 *Student Learning Data* *Student Think-Alouds*	*Student Conversations*	*Teachers will record anecdotal comments while listening to students' conversations and thinking aloud with a partner during the months of November and December (aim to collect notes on five students per week)*

(Continued)

Table 4.1 (Continued)

What evidence is going to be collected?	How is the evidence going to be collected?	When is the evidence going to be collected? By whom?
Data Source 3 *Student Learning Data/Perceptual Data (depending on the prompt)* *Student Reflections*	*Exit Cards*	*English, science, and history teachers will collect exit cards once every two weeks from October to December. Prompts might include the following:* *How do you go about explaining your opinion?* *How do you convey your message clearly when sharing your opinion?* *How does the think-aloud strategy work for you?* *Note: Teachers to ensure cards are dated.*

Evidence of Implementation of Practice:

Checklist developed for effective think-alouds

Anchor charts (hanging in classrooms)

Opinion prompts given to students

Think-aloud scripts (developed by teachers)

Daybook evidence showing number of times teachers engaged in a think-aloud

Evidence documenting number of times students engaged in a think-aloud

Team members agreed to try their first think-aloud that week so that they could discuss it when the team came together the following week. As the school year progressed, the team continued to meet weekly. During the weekly meetings, teachers shared and discussed the various prompts they developed for students in an effort to refine them, continued to write think-aloud scripts, discussed ways that they could assess students' conversations, shared how they were gradually releasing responsibility to the students, examined student work, and held one another accountable for implementation. In late December, the team decided it was time to examine the collected evidence to answer their inquiry question.

CONSIDERING IMPLEMENTATION

Over the years, researchers have identified strategies that have a greater impact on student learning. However, even strategies that have been shown to be highly effective (e.g., think-alouds) may not be so powerful to impact student achievement the first time teachers try them. Teachers are "beginning users" the first time they try to implement a strategy, and it is likely that they will be less effective at executing it than if they had used it many times before.

As mentioned earlier, teams must not only consider the evidence related to the student learning need that was collected, but also the evidence related to the implementation of practice. If teachers did not use the strategy regularly and effectively, it would be impractical to examine the effects of that strategy on student learning. Having said that, facilitators must recognize that not all teachers are going to be an expert at executing the strategy the first time they try it. Considering the implementation of the strategies identified at a classroom, team, and school level will help the team in considering next steps.

Activity 12—Levels of Implementation

> Materials Needed: Levels of Implementation Templates (Resource H)

Before the team considers evidence of student learning, they should consider levels of implementation of the teacher action identified in their inquiry question. Distribute the Levels of Implementation Template—Classroom (Resource H).

Figure 4.2 Levels of Implementation Template

Levels of Implementation Template (Classroom)			
What does deep implementation of _____ look like in the classroom?			
Beginning Level	**Developing Level**	**Applying Level**	**Innovating Level**

What marks the separation between the developing level of implementation and the applying level is the consideration of impact. When teachers consider how the strategy impacts student learning and use this information to inform their practice, they move from developing to applying levels of implementation.

If your team developed an Innovation Configuration Map, it would be helpful to refer to it to help guide the discussion.

Individuals can use this template to consider levels of implementation at a classroom level and reflect on the implementation of the teacher action identified in their inquiry question. Begin with the column labeled "Applying Level." Explain that at the applying level, teachers are able to use the strategy proficiently. Ask the team to describe the indicators that would show the teacher is proficient at a level of basic implementation. Next, proceed to the column labeled "Innovating Level," and ask the team to describe the indicators that would show the team is at an advanced level and into deep implementation. The team can then address the columns labeled "Developing Level" and "Beginning Level." Once the template is complete, ask teachers to consider their current level of implementation.

Vignette—A Professional Learning Community in Action Continued

The following implementation continuum was developed by the teachers at Main Street Public School:

What does deep implementation of think-aloud look like in the classroom?

Table 4.2   Implementation of a Think-Aloud

Beginning Level	Developing Level	Applying Level	Innovating Level
Teachers think aloud but often move in and out of the role of the learner while doing so—switching between thinking aloud and	*Teachers are using the checklist developed to guide their think-aloud. Teachers explain what students should look for and debrief after*	*Teachers have internalized the important aspects of the think-aloud and have become more efficient in preparing them. Teachers select the area of focus based*	*During the think-aloud, teachers not only share how they select strategies and fix problems encountered but they also share*

Beginning Level	Developing Level	Applying Level	Innovating Level
questioning students. Teachers do not always tell students what to look for prior to the think-aloud and occasionally forget to debrief. *The students' role is to listen. Students are guided by the teacher through similar situations to practice the skill that was focused on during the think-aloud.*	*thinking aloud. Lengthy think-alouds are becoming shorter—with greater focus. Teachers concentrate on one skill and share strategies with students.* *Students are provided opportunities to practice skills in small groups.*	*on assessment of student learning and the identified needs of the students. Not only do teachers share strategies, they share problems in their thinking and demonstrate how they, as learners, cope when they encounter a problem in their learning.* *Students are provided opportunities to think aloud—sharing their thoughts and strategies with each other.*	*how they monitor their understanding.* *Teachers are collaboratively considering how think-aloud impacts student learning and working to adapt the approach in other contexts.* *Students are provided with multiple opportunities to make their thinking visible along with opportunities to examine how strategies advance their understanding.*

Next, facilitators may decide to engage the team in reflecting on the level of implementation at the team and school level depending on individuals' levels of implementation. The purpose of identifying deep implementation among the team and within the school is to have the team consider next steps in developing consistency of practice. If team members reached applying and innovating levels of implementation, they may be ready to devise strategies to spread the practices further throughout the building. The Levels of Implementation Templates—Collaborative Inquiry Team and Entire Staff (Resource H) can be completed as a means to guide this discussion.

Teams should consider levels of implementation in relation to all other evidence gathered. If efforts were abandoned prior to deep implementation, teams need to consider how much confidence they can place in the data before moving to analysis.

DATA ANALYSIS

Step 1—Organizing the Data

> "Professional expertise is not just having the evidence or being aware of it. It's also about knowing how to judge the evidence and knowing what to do with it." (Hargreaves & Fullan, 2012, p. 54)

This step involves managing and organizing the data collected for your team's inquiry. Before your team can begin to interpret the data collected, it must first be put in to a form that will facilitate analysis. Organizing the data may include the following: ensuring that it has been dated and labeled (e.g., applied science, applied English), sequencing the data, making copies so that pages can be marked up, and ensuring it is legible. Data from each data source should be prepared separately.

Vignette—A Professional Learning Community in Action Continued

The facilitator of the intermediate teachers' collaborative inquiry at Main Street Public School gathered the following evidence from the team one week prior to the date set to analyze data:

- Journals of the three marker students
- Teachers' anecdotal notes regarding student conversations
- Exit cards

After checking to ensure dates were included on each of these items and labeling them according to subject area, the facilitator placed them in chronological order and then proceeded to make copies of each item. One copy was made for each teacher on the team.

> In the previous example, the data sources related to student learning included student work products (written response to opinion prompts collected via journals), students' conversations (collected via anecdotal notes recorded by the teacher), and student reflections (collected via exit card).

Organizing the data for your team will help facilitate analysis. Dating and labeling (history—Period 2, history—Period 3, etc.) the data from each source separately might not seem important ahead of time, but it may lead to some insights later in the process. The team should collectively determine the timeline for analyzing the data and set a date for which the analysis will occur. While facilitators should organize the data less than a week from the date set for analysis, it would be helpful to check with teachers periodically to ensure they are not experiencing difficulties collecting what was outlined in the plan. If they fall behind schedule, timelines should be adjusted accordingly.

Step 2—Reading the Data

Materials Needed: Data (after it has been organized), Highlighters

Members of the team need to become familiar with the data. This entails reading it numerous times. To start, ask team members to consider each individual data source and consider what it might mean. While reading the evidence, participants may want to record their initial thoughts in the margins or highlight sections or issues that seem important. In addition to recording initial impressions, teachers will also begin to search for recurring themes and common details.

Step 3—Describing the Data

During this step, teams describe the data. It helps if team members bring objectivity to this step, as at this point, teams are not familiar enough with the evidence to move into interpretation. Facilitators should ask the team to consider each data source separately. Individuals reread the data and compose three to five factual statements related to the evidence.

This step could be done individually prior to coming together as a team to engage in Step 3—describing the data. By engaging in the reading independently, team members will bring their unique perspectives to the next step. Facilitators might also decide to distribute different data sources to individuals on the team (e.g., student journals to two people, anecdotal notes to two people, and exit cards to two people). This decision may be based on practicality (e.g., there may be more data than time required for analysis). Even so, this can be a strategy for triangulating data if common themes are found by individuals examining different data sources.

Possible Prompts: Review the evidence. What do you see? Avoid interpretation. Share factual statements only. Just the facts! If you catch yourself using *because— therefore—it seems—however,* then stop! Just describe what is in front of you.

Activity 13—Fact or Interpretation?

To ensure that participants know and understand the difference between fact and interpretation, facilitators might engage team members in the following activity. Stand and ask participants to use factual statements only to describe your physical appearance. One person might begin by saying you are tall, for example. This statement is not a fact—it is interpretive. Whenever someone uses statements that contain an interpretation, be sure to call it to the attention of the group—accept factual statements only. Other examples of interpretive statements might include, you dress nice, you are stylish, you like to wear your hair up, you like to wear blue, you prefer pantsuits to skirts, and so on. Examples of factual statements might include, you are more than 5 feet tall, your blouse is navy blue, your hair is pulled off your face with a ribbon, and your pants and jacket have the same pattern and are made of the same material. Engaging in this activity will help individuals remain objective in their descriptions of the evidence related to their inquiry.

Vignette—A Professional Learning Community in Action Continued

The following are statements of fact and interpretation related to the collaborative inquiry conducted by the teachers at Main Street Public School.

Facts

- The students' journals contain responses to 12 different opinion prompts.
- Students wrote at least three sentences for each prompt.
- Students engaged in their own think-aloud at least once in each subject area (history, science, and English).
- Fifteen students stated an opinion in the first sentence of each journal response entry. One of the 18 marker students argued for both sides in more than half of his journal responses. Two of the 18 marker students argued for both sides in a third of their journal responses.
- Students used an explanation to support reasons more often than they used a statistic or an analogy.

The statements contained in the first set objectively relate to the facts alone. The second set of examples show subjectivity rooted in assumptions. The statements may not be founded in the evidence.

Interpretation

- The opinion prompts were well designed in each of the three subject areas.
- Students enjoy thinking aloud while engaging in conversations with classmates.
- Most students' opinions are well supported.
- Students do not understand the difference between a fact and an opinion.
- Students do not value statistics.

To ensure that participants stay focused on the facts, facilitators might offer the following sentence starters during this step in data analysis:

- I observe that . . .
- I see. . . .
- I can count. . . .
- There are . . .

Next, facilitators ask individuals to take turns sharing factual statements for each data source. Describing the evidence in this manner enhances and leads to Step 4—classifying the data.

Step 4—Classifying the Data

Materials Needed: Highlighters

Qualitative data analysis is a process of breaking down data into smaller units. In this step, the team identifies themes and develops a coding system that will allow the team to group the data. The typical way qualitative data are broken down is through the process of coding or classifying. A category is a classification of ideas or concepts. When concepts in the data are examined and compared to one another and connections are made, categories are formed. Categories are used to organize similar concepts into distinct groups.

During this step, facilitators lead teams in developing a coding system so that they can identify themes. Coding the data sources allows teams to identify patterns related to data from different times or from different sources. Once the big patterns have been identified, other smaller patterns will emerge as the process continues. It is important that all members of the team have the same understanding of the meanings attached to the codes. In the end, all members must determine what codes they will use—not only for the purpose of consistency, but so they have an understanding of the codes attached to the themes identified.

Vignette—A Professional Learning Community in Action Continued

One way the Main Street Public School team decided to classify its data was according to the type of support students provided to back their reasons. They assigned the following codes to the data:

A   Analogies/Comparisons

S   Statistic

E Example (this category was further broken down)

E–PE an example based on personal experience

E–VE an example based on vicarious experience

EO Expert Opinion

EA Emotional Appeals

O Other

In doing so, the team discovered that many students supported reasons using the *same* type of support modeled by teachers during the think-aloud shared in class that day with the exception of analogies. For example, if teachers modeled using a statistic, the students also used a statistic as the type of support to back the reason given for *their* opinion. When teachers modeled the use of analogy, very few students chose this type of support to back their reasons. This was evident in all subject areas in both the journal responses and students' think-alouds. The team also discovered that in the students' think-alouds, on days when teachers did not provide a model, most students used an example based on personal experience to back their reason.

Another way the team decided to classify its data was based on the prompt given. Prompts along with students' responses to those prompts were categorized according to the following coding scheme:

EXP Prompts that explicitly stated, "Provide an opinion, reason, and support."

IMP Prompts that implicitly asked for students' opinions.

The following is an example of a prompt that included explicit instructions given by the science teachers: Do you think that damage to the environment is a consequence of worldwide improvements in the standard of living? State your opinion, provide convincing reasons, and support for your choice. Examples of opinion prompts that were not explicit included these questions: If you could change one major historical event, what would it be? Do you believe the city you live in is supportive of racial diversity?

By classifying the data this way, the team discovered differences in the responses given by students based on the prompt. Most of the students provided reasons and support for the reason when it was explicitly stated in the prompt. About half of the students did not when the opinion prompt was implicit. In cross-referencing this information with other records of student data, the team noted that of the students experiencing difficulty when prompted implicitly, most also experienced difficulty inferring.

As facilitators assist teams in coding the data, ensure that the team takes the time to consider possible classifications that might lead to new insights. Once the data are classified, it is important that the team reviews it and reduces it by discarding irrelevant information. In doing so, the team considers the following for each theme identified:

- Is the theme reflected in more than one data source?
- Are smaller patterns contained within the themes? If so, what are they?
- On closer inspection, what evidence is not a good fit?
- On closer inspection, what evidence best represents each theme identified?

Step 5—Interpreting the Data

In the final step of data analysis, teams form conclusions and determine the implications of their findings. During this step, as team members attach meaning and significance, they determine what is important. In interpreting the evidence, collaborative inquiry teams consider the following:

- What does the evidence tell us about our inquiry question?
- What assumptions did we make about students and their learning?
- What are some things we could do to deal with this?
- What are the strengths and weaknesses we see based on the data?

Activity 14—Drawing Conclusions

> Materials Needed: Team's Inquiry Question—posted, Blank Index Cards, Two Talking Chips per team member (talking chips may be tokens or coins)

The purpose of this activity is to draw conclusions from participants. Talking chips are used as a way to manage the discussion so that every participant has a chance to contribute. Distribute one blank index card and two talking chips to each participant. To assist teams in interpreting the evidence, refer to the group's inquiry question (posted in the room) and restate it so that group members hear it. Ask teachers to consider what the evidence tells them about the inquiry question. Provide a few minutes for individuals to reflect quietly, encouraging them to record their thoughts and ideas on the blank index card. Once ideas have been generated independently, invite teachers to share their thoughts with the larger team. As a participant shares a thought, he places one talking chip in the center of the table. Participants might refer to what they recorded on their index cards or build on one another's ideas. Once all chips have been placed in the center, participants remove their chips and repeat the process. Facilitators end the activity when they feel the team has drawn conclusions that consider all evidence.

Facilitators either record statements or ask a team member to record the dialogue during the exercise. To ensure everyone on the team agrees with the conclusions drawn, facilitators reread each statement and ask team members to clarify, question, and/or expand as necessary.

> Artifact: This information should be saved as documentation of the team's learning as the team might consider sharing it with a wider audience in Stage 4—documenting, sharing, and celebrating.

Vignette—A Professional Learning Community in Action Continued

Based on their inquiry question, what is the impact of the think-aloud strategy on students' ability to share opinions with detailed and relevant reasons accompanied by clear and sufficient support and the coded data, teachers from Main Street Public School offered the following statements during the talking-chip exercise:

"The evidence tells us that the marker students improved."

"The evidence tells us that all teachers shared their thinking aloud with their class to demonstrate how to support an opinion."

"The evidence tells us that the quality of students' responses depended on the prompts we provided."

"The evidence tells us that when we were explicit in asking students to provide reasons and support, they were more likely to do so."

"The evidence tells us that students used personal experiences more than other types of support when backing their opinions."

"The evidence tells us that descriptive feedback helped students improve the quality of their responses."

The team continued to use the talking chips as a structure to share their interpretations of the evidence. The statements that were recorded during the talking-chip activity were used to develop the following summary:

The think-aloud is an effective strategy for teaching intermediate students how to form and support an opinion. Within two months, each marker student moved up a minimum of two levels on the achievement chart. In addition to the think-aloud, opinion prompts impacted student learning. When explicitly asked for their opinion, students were more likely to state their opinion, provide detailed and relevant reasons for their opinions, and provide support for their reason. For prompts where an opinion was implicitly called for, about half of the students failed to provide sufficient support for reasons. The most frequent type of support students provided was personal experiences and the least frequent type of support used were comparisons or analogies. Every student indicated that the think-aloud strategy helped support their learning.

In addition, the team agreed on the following:

- Teachers' and students' understanding and use of think-alouds increased.
- Teachers and students' understanding of how to form and support an opinion increased.
- Levels of implementation varied from one classroom to the next.
- With practice, teachers and students became more effective developing and using think-alouds.
- When students were given opportunities to work with partners prior to working independently, the quality of their work increased.

EXAMINING ASSUMPTIONS

Next, facilitators engage the team in examining assumptions. Assumptions are beliefs or ideas that people hold to be true. These beliefs guide people's actions. As mentioned earlier, meeting adaptive challenges requires reconception of the very paradigm in which one is working (Vander Ark, 2006), and therefore, educators must not only change their traditional practices but they must also consider the assumptions that drive those practices (DuFour, DuFour, Eaker, & Karhanek, 2010). While one cannot help but make assumptions,

"But before I join the chorus of 'this too shall pass' and vow to wait out the next administrative requirement, I must turn the lens inward and ask the question every true professional must ask: 'Is my present practice as effective as I think it is?' As teachers, we must be willing to confront this question every day of our professional lives if teacher leadership is to become a reality rather than a slogan." (Reeves, 2008, p. 50) one can deliberately examine whether they are rational and reasonable. Stage 3 of collaborative inquiry—analyzing evidence—culminates with teams revisiting and revising their theories of action.

Hattie (2012) noted that theories have purposes as tools for synthesizing notions, but teachers often maintain their theories even when the evidence of impact does not support particular theories. Theories are wired in by years of habit. Hattie suggests, "Evidence of impact *or not* [italics added] may mean that teachers need to modify or dramatically change their theories of action" (p. 4). During this activity, facilitators engage teams in testing assumptions in their theories of action by articulating assumptions and asking for confirming or disconfirming evidence.

Activity 15—Uncovering Assumptions

Materials Needed: Collaborative Inquiry Team's Theory of Action

Facilitators ask the team to revisit the causal statements in their theory of action. In light of the team's interpretation of the evidence collected, ask the team to consider what holds true in their theory and what might require a revision.

Possible Prompts: Consider the if-then statements in the theory of action. Based on the evidence we collected and analyzed, what changes do we need to make to our theory? What assumptions did we make about students and their learning? Have those assumptions changed? What is the confirming or disconfirming evidence?

Vignette—A Professional Learning Community in Action Continued

When considering what assumptions were made about students and their learning and what things they could do to deal with those assumptions, the team reconsidered its theory of action. Upon doing so, the team realized that their theory contained inaccuracies and was incomplete. The team thoughtfully examined each statement and revised as necessary. As they did so, they asked themselves about the effect they were having on student learning.

Original Statement 1

If we engage in collaborative inquiry focusing on supporting opinions across different content areas, *then* students will have a better understanding of how to effectively support an opinion.

When reflecting on the first statement, the team realized that because of engaging in the inquiry, not only did students gain a better understanding of how to effectively support an opinion, but teachers did as well.

An assumption contained in this statement is that content-area teachers were in support of and equipped to teach students how to learn to write. When revisiting this statement, one of the science teachers admitted that when they began their inquiry he had a difficult time seeing a fit within his curriculum. He had been used to having students make predictions and form hypothesis but rarely asked students to share their opinions. He struggled seeing how this was going to advance his content-area goals and was not sure how he could assess students' knowledge and understanding of scientific concepts based on opinion prompts. He exposed to the team that he was a bit resentful in the beginning due to the fact that he felt that it was the English teacher's responsibility to teach students how to write an opinion.

The science teacher admitted that, as the inquiry progressed and with support from the team, he began to see the impact the work was having on student learning and as a result decided to try it in his class. Based on their work together, the two science teachers realized three things. First, tasks that asked students to form and support opinions provided high-level cognitive processing opportunities for students in science. Second, by outlining success criteria for the learning target (based on curriculum) and separating it from instructions on how to successfully complete the task (forming and supporting an opinion), the teachers were able to see how they could use an opinion prompt to assess content area knowledge. Finally, the two teachers concluded that opinion prompts were an effective way to reveal students' knowledge and understanding about scientific concepts. Based on this discussion, the team revised their theory.

Revised Statement 1

If we engage in collaborative inquiry focusing on supporting opinions across different content areas, *then* students and *teachers* will have a better understanding of how to effectively support an opinion. *In addition, students will be provided with opportunities to demonstrate their knowledge and understanding of the content using complex learning tasks.*

Original Statement 2

If we use the think-aloud strategy, *then* students will hear our thought processes as we provide reasons and support for our opinions.

This statement assumes that teachers know how to engage in a think-aloud. Conversation revolved around how teachers initially struggled putting themselves in the role of the learner and *remaining* in that role as they progressed through the think-aloud. In the beginning, teachers found themselves moving back and forth—at times explaining what they were doing rather than explaining how they were thinking through the process. After discussing the progress, they remained in the role of the learner through practice; the team decided that the second statement did not need to be revised. The team was pleased that they now shared a common understanding of the think-aloud strategy and felt they were more effective in using it as a strategy to increase student learning.

Original Statement 3

If we provide opportunities for students to respond to opinion prompts regularly, *then* they will get better with practice.

Upon revisiting the third statement, the team was reminded of the importance of providing descriptive feedback. Teachers agreed that descriptive feedback was pivotal in increasing students' understanding and moving them up the levels of the achievement chart. They revised their third statement to include this realization.

Revised Statement 3

If we provide opportunities for students to respond to opinion prompts regularly *and provide them with descriptive feedback, then* they will get better with practice.

Original Statement 4

If we monitor the work of three marker students each, *then* our actions will be better informed.

The team agreed that monitoring of the three marker students did not take place regularly. The team felt that if they had monitored more frequently, they could have used the information to guide their instruction on a day-to-day basis. Teachers agreed that they would have encouraged students to use more comparisons and analogies to support their reasons. Team members agreed that had they increased their use of formative assessments they would have helped students make connections between explicit and implicit opinion prompts.

Revised Statement 4

If we *frequently* monitor the work of three marker students each *and use that information to guide our instruction, then we can be more responsive to the needs of the students.*

Original Statement 5

If we provide opportunities for students to think aloud while pairing with another student, *then* they will further improve because of having heard their classmate's thinking.

The team agreed that this statement assumed that students were prepared to engage in think-alouds. As teachers implemented the strategy in their classrooms, they realized that they needed to gradually release responsibility to students. The team also realized that providing opportunities for students to think aloud was not enough. Co-constructing anchor charts and success criteria were important aspects as well.

The teachers examined their purpose in pairing students and acknowledged that by providing students with success criteria, students would not only be able to listen to one another thinking aloud, they would be able to use the success criteria to engage in peer and self-assessment.

Revised Statement 5

If we provide opportunities for students to think aloud while pairing with another student *and guide their use of anchor charts and success criteria for the purpose of peer and self-assessment, then* they will further improve because of having heard their classmate's thinking and having to *provide feedback to one another.*

Original Statement 6

If we meet regularly to share our learning, *then* we will be more likely to be open and transparent about the challenges we are facing.

The team acknowledged how they had progressed in deprivatizing their practice because of engaging in collaborative inquiry. They all agreed that taking a learning stance and focusing on description that was free of judgment helped to foster open and honest communication in which team members felt safe to share challenges.

Hattie (2012) suggests, "The most powerful way of thinking about a teacher's role is for teachers to see themselves as *evaluators* of their effects on students. Teachers need to use evidence-based methods to inform, change, and sustain these evaluation beliefs about their effect. These beliefs relate to claims about what each student can do as a consequence of the teacher's actions, and how every resource (especially peers) can be used to play a part in moving students from what they can do now to where the teacher considers they should be—and to do so in the most efficient, as well as effective manner" (p. 14). As teams revisit and revise the causal statements in their theory of action, they are evaluating *their* effect on learning while confronting their beliefs and assumptions that impact student achievement.

Heifetz (1994) described how adaptive challenges require people to make a shift in their values and habits. By revisiting the team's theory of action, facilitators engage teachers in examining their beliefs and help them identify those that work and question those that do not work well. This exercise will help to provide reasons to change behaviors that are incongruent with what is valued. Once the underlying reasons of why teachers believe what they do are understood, it makes it easier for them to defend the professional choices they make.

> "In collaborative cultures, failure and uncertainty are not protected and defended, but instead are shared and discussed with a view to gaining help and support."
> (Hargreaves & Fullan, 2012, p. 113)

Activity 16—Considering Strengths and Weaknesses

As a final step, facilitators ask teams to consider strengths and weaknesses based on the data.

Vignette—A Professional Learning Community in Action Continued

In considering strengths and weaknesses based on the data, the team felt they had learned a lot about how to help students form and support an opinion. They felt a sense of collective efficacy based on the results of their hard work. They agreed that it was easier to assess students' written responses than it was to assess students' conversations. The team noted that had they developed a tool to assess students' conversations, they would place greater confidence in the anecdotal evidence collected to assess students' thinking. They listed the creation of a tool to assess conversations as an action item for their team.

The group then launched into a discussion about strategies for evaluating arguments and types of support wondering if certain types of support were more sufficient than others and wondering how they could assist students in making comparisons and developing analogies as a means to support reasons for their opinions. The team also wondered how they might help students share opinions with detailed and relevant reasons accompanied by clear and sufficient support even when this information is not explicitly stated in a prompt.

Ask the team to identify strengths and weaknesses based on the data. This will provide the scaffold needed in determining next steps (Stage 4).

Possible Prompts: Did we measure what we thought we were measuring? Were our measures reliable? Did we use a variety of data sources? Were the data sources appropriately matched to our question? Was there a better way to collect the evidence than the way our team went about it? What were the strengths and weaknesses of the data we used for our inquiry? Could we have improved as far as data collection?

Now that teams have completed the third stage of the collaborative inquiry cycle (analyzing evidence), they should be ready to document and share their conclusions with a wider audience and celebrate their learning.

In the fourth and final stage (documenting, sharing, and celebrating), teams consolidate and share their learning, determine next steps, and debrief the process.

REFLECTION FOR FACILITATORS

Facilitators should refer back to their previous assessments of their skills as effective facilitators determined at the conclusion of Chapters 2 and 3. Before moving to Stage 4 (documenting, sharing, and celebrating), facilitators are encouraged to reflect on an additional five skills and approaches. The areas for growth identified through this reflection could be used to maintain a focus while facilitating teams throughout the final stage of collaborative inquiry.

Table 4.3   Reflection for Facilitators

Facilitator Skills and Approaches	Level 1	Level 2	Level 3	Level 4
Uses participant experiences, work samples, dilemmas as material for examination	Beginning	Developing	Applying	Innovating
Uses varied and appropriate structures to maximize participation and ensure that all voices are heard	Beginning	Developing	Applying	Innovating
Persists in the face of group discomfort—focuses on it during reflective periods	Beginning	Developing	Applying	Innovating
Addresses conflict when it arises	Beginning	Developing	Applying	Innovating
Is transparent about reasoning behind many decisions made by facilitator	Beginning	Developing	Applying	Innovating

Source: Adapted from National School Reform Faculty: New York: Facilitation Standards.

Stage 4

Documenting, Celebrating, and Sharing

You give people the room to adapt, based on their experience and exper-tise. All you ask is that they talk to one another and take responsibility. That is what works.

(Gawande, 2009, p. 73)

In the fourth stage, collaborative inquiry teams document, share, and celebrate their journey. Documenting the work is an important part of the process because it helps the team to articulate and clarify thoughts, making it a crucial part of learning from the inquiry. Sharing experiences about how the team worked through an educational concern will help others in recognizing the benefits of engaging in the process. Through celebration, efforts are acknowledged and team members become motivated to engage in the next cycle of inquiry. Finally, the process is debriefed to further develop the team and provide direction for the future. Contained in this chapter are prompts and activities that facilitators can use to guide participants through each of these processes.

DOCUMENTING AND SHARING

At this point in the process, teams have formulated conclusions relating to their inquiries. During Stage 4, teams decide on a format for documenting and sharing their findings with a wider audience. In addition, teams

> "The challenges are difficult as teacher leaders strive to achieve widespread implementation of action research. The goals will require a commitment of time for research, public sharing of results, and personal reflection." (Reeves, 2008, p. 45)

determine recommendations and consider next steps. Documenting the work not only concludes the collaborative inquiry cycle, it also encourages further reflection and helps consolidate understanding. Participants are empowered as they recognize that they are not only capable of applying knowledge but also of producing it, fueling a desire to continue to assess their impact and improve student learning.

In addition, documenting the team's inquiry provides a record of the link between the actions of teachers and school leaders (causes) and student results (effects). Hattie (2012) notes, "Teachers must be vigilant as to the consequences for learning based on their classroom climate, their teaching, and their students' co-teaching and co-learning" (p. 17). Hattie also shared how schools in New Zealand earn greater autonomy if they are able to show evidence of "having dependable systems about their impact" (p. 153) stating, "The reward is teachers knowing, in a dependable and public manner, the quality of their impact" (p. 153). Reeves (2010) also noted that in systems where cause and effect data are examined and the link between the actions of teachers and student results is documented in a clear and public way, replication of mistakes is unlikely. Documentation of the team's inquiry will not only provide a means of sharing findings with interested others but will serve as public record of the link between professional development, the implementation of strategies, and student results. This information will be instrumental in helping schools move forward in meeting their goal of increasing learning and achieving greater success for *all* students.

Formats for sharing range from formal research reports to less formal products such as scrapbooks, timelines, storyboards, videos, and documentation panels (three-panel displays that can be folded shut or displayed open). Depending on the audience, teams might decide to document their collaborative inquiry in different ways. When facilitators allow choice in documenting inquiries, it fosters creativity and demonstrates that they honor the team's professional judgment.

Documentation, however, is not meant to be an onerous process. If facilitators follow the suggestions in this book, much of the work should already be completed. Teams only need to determine the best way to share their learning and transfer the artifacts collected during the cycle, along with additional reflections and considerations of where to go next, into the format of their choice. If the work becomes unmanageable for individuals during this final stage, facilitators run the risk of deflecting time and energy away from what really matters—addressing student learning needs. To ensure the completion of the final product is distributed among the team, facilitators might suggest that individuals take responsibility for certain components. While encouraging teams to be creative in how they document and share their information, facilitators might suggest that certain components are included. These key components are outlined here.

DOCUMENTING COLLABORATIVE INQUIRY—KEY COMPONENTS

Identifying Information. Include the names of team members and the name of the school.

Collaborative Inquiry Question. Sharing the final version of the team's inquiry question will help to further set the context for the audience. Teams might also include various versions of the question and share how their thinking evolved as they proceeded through the process and revised the question accordingly.

Shared Vision. During Stage 1, teams developed a shared vision by painting a picture of their preferred future or crafting a destination postcard. Including the team's shared vision will assist the audience in understanding the team's aspirations and hopes for the students in their school. It will also serve as a helpful reminder for the team as they consider their next steps.

Rationale and/or Purpose Statement. Teams should be encouraged to share the rationale for their inquiry, as it will help the audience understand why the inquiry was worth conducting. The audience needs to be invited to think about the problem and its implications for students and learning.

Possible Prompts: How did the idea originate? Why was it important to the team? How was it linked to the team's preferred future? What was the purpose of the team's inquiry?

Theory of Action. Since the team's theory of action can be thought of as "a story line that makes a vision and a strategy concrete" (City, Elmore, Fiarman, & Teitel, 2009, p. 40), including the theory will help the audience to understand the team's thinking related to the actions and strategies chosen. It may also serve as documentation of how teams adapted to meet the challenges faced along the way.

Description of the Actions Taken. The report should contain some description of the actions taken to address the student learning needs identified.

The team might also include the reasons particular strategies were chosen along with reflections regarding implementation.

Findings and Conclusions. Collaborative inquiry should result in educators coming to a new understanding about how to support student learning. Therefore, documentation should contain some description of what the team learned. During Stage 3, facilitators led teams in forming conclusions (Activity 14). The statements recorded during this activity could be shared with the audience and expanded if necessary.

Recommendations and Next Steps. The final key component that collaborative inquiry teams should include in their documentation is recommendations and next steps. If the team has not yet considered recommendations and next steps, facilitators should encourage them to do so at this point.

> *Possible Prompts:* How can we apply what we learned to further actions? What will those future actions include and how can we collect evidence on the next set of actions? What are the most urgent, emerging student learning needs? What do we still need to learn about?

If participants have not gained new insights about the problem, it is likely that they are only summarizing and not reflecting at this stage. Reflection is a powerful learning experience and an essential part of collaborative inquiry. Encourage the team to reflect on both the professional learning and student learning while reviewing the conclusions that were recorded during Activity 14. Most important, this section should answer the following two questions: What are the implications of this work for student learning? What are the implications of this work for teacher learning?

Once teams have completed documenting their inquiries, they will need the time and opportunity to share it with others. For teams who might be interested, facilitators could seek opportunities for participants to publish their work in journals or present it at conferences. Opportunities for sharing with the school community and parent councils should be readily available. Additionally, celebrations provide an opportunity for teams to share their learning and are an important aspect of the final stage of collaborative inquiry. Considerations for organizing celebrations are presented in the section that follows.

CELEBRATING

In addition to documenting the collaborative inquiry, during the fourth stage, it is important for facilitators to ensure that teams celebrate their journey. While ultimately, the end goal is to increase learning and achieve greater success for *all* students, one purpose for celebrating is to motivate people to continue regardless if teams found evidence of impact at a student achievement level or not. Acknowledging the effort of the team and celebrating the professional learning that occurred because of the collaborative inquiry process will make people feel respected and want to continue. It may even result in increased participation as individuals who have never experienced the process witness the camaraderie and as a result, desire to become part of it.

In addition, celebrations signal what is important and reinforce shared values (DuFour, 1998). Noting the importance of celebrating as an effective strategy for shaping the culture of an organization, DuFour (1998) suggested that celebrations fuel momentum by "calling attention to the presence of behaviors consistent with the school's values" (p. 59), helping to reinforce improvement initiatives. By engaging teams in a celebration, facilitators honor the teams' collective efforts while reinforcing collaborative inquiry as an empowering approach for considering the impact of adult actions on student outcomes.

Another reason to celebrate is to make evident the accomplishments that resulted from teamwork. Marzano, Waters, and McNulty (2005) pointed out, "Teachers tend to operate from the perspective that their contribution to student learning is more a function of their individual efforts than the collective efforts of the staff" (p. 101). Celebration will help to highlight the power of working as a team and develop collective efficacy (a shared belief that together, we can make a difference). Marzano et al. (2005) suggested that recognizing and celebrating accomplishments helps "create the collective efficacy that typifies a purposeful community" (p. 101). Although not every team will be able to document evidence of impact on student learning, participants will increase their awareness of which teaching strategies are working well and which strategies are not working well. Through celebration, participants will recognize that together, they are one step closer to achieving greater success for *all* students.

Celebrations can take many shapes and forms—from large learning fairs consisting of teams from schools across the district to smaller events where one team comes together at the end of the cycle. The scale of the celebration will depend on the time and resources available. There are a number of things to consider when planning for a celebration including audience and format for sharing.

If time and resources allow, it would be advantageous to network collaborative inquiry teams from different schools and across different panels (elementary schools and secondary schools). One of the strengths of collaborative inquiry as an approach to professional learning is that it recognizes the role of teachers as agents of change. Bringing teams together for sharing would expand opportunities for teachers to learn from and with one another, further honoring their expertise and professionalism. A protocol for sharing in this environment has been included (Resource I). Facilitators might also consider including various stakeholders in the celebration. The celebration may be an opportunity to build home, school, and community relationships. Also, facilitators should ask teams to consider student's voices. Is there an opportunity to bring students into the celebration? If so, what meaningful role could students play in sharing?

To plan for a successful celebration, facilitators will also need to know the format teams selected for sharing. As mentioned earlier, there are many ways teams can share their learning, and it is best if they are given a choice in how to do so. Whether teams chose a written report, scrapbook, or video format, the requirements should not result in onerous work. Awareness of the format will enable facilitators to gather the equipment necessary for sharing (e.g., data projector, laptop, and speakers would be required for teams who produced a video).

Most important, however, whatever shape, facilitators must ensure the authenticity of the celebration. As part of the celebration entails sharing, having knowledge of the team's inquiry and conclusions drawn, and structuring activities to ensure full participation of all team members will help facilitators create an event that is meaningful and rewarding for participants. While celebrating and sharing go hand in hand, it is important that during the event, the team be recognized for the work in which they engaged. Facilitators are encouraged to find creative ways to honor teams during the celebration. Certificates of participation and applause are a couple of ideas that work well.

DEBRIEFING THE PROCESS

At this point, facilitators have engaged teams in reflecting on the impact of their actions on student outcomes, professional learning, and student learning. In the final stage of collaborative inquiry, facilitators engage teams in further reflection by debriefing the process. This is an important final step as debriefing will not only bring closure to the process, it will help provide a way for facilitators to further develop the team and give direction for the future. It also helps the team recognize how the process can be useful in tackling adaptive challenges and building adaptive capacity.

Adaptive challenges require new learning. Determining appropriate solutions to adaptive problems requires that the individuals with the problem experiment with different ways of doing things and challenge established ways of thinking. Individuals must adapt to meet the difficult challenges. Collaborative inquiry provides a structure that supports individuals in adapting. Individually and collectively, participants take on the gradual process of figuring out new ways that build from the best of what was done in the past. In doing so, long-standing fundamental beliefs are examined and new values are adopted. Many characteristics of collaborative inquiry play a critical role in helping team members build adaptive capacity. These characteristics are outlined next.

The process is collaborative.

Collaborative inquiry requires participants to collectively dissect their experiences. Each team member's contribution brings new insights to understanding the problem. The diverse skills, backgrounds, and experiences each member contributes helps individuals consider alternative perspectives. Consideration of alternative perspectives helps to fuel learning and contributes to problem

> "Organized groups provide the social interaction that often deepens learning and the interpersonal support and synergy necessary for creatively solving the complex problems of teaching and learning." (Crow, ed., 2011, p. 26)

solving. When debriefing the process, it is important for facilitators to engage the team in considering how well they worked together, if they honored diversity, along with how to enhance the team's effectiveness.

The process is reflective.

Reflection helps to increase recognition of professional dilemmas. One of the four essential issues concerning reflection identified by Halton and Smith (1995) was that we learn to frame and reframe complex or ambiguous problems, test various interpretations, and then modify our actions consequently. Critical aspects of addressing adaptive challenges will lead to discarding entrenched ways and generating the knowledge and competencies required to do things differently. When debriefing the process, it is important for facilitators to engage individuals in considering how reflection contributed to their learning.

Engagement requires that participants take a learning stance.

Collaborative inquiry requires participants to interrogate classroom practices that have been traditionally private while assuming the role of a learner. Katz (2010) described the

> "Through exploration of individual and collective experiences, learners actively construct, analyze, evaluate, and synthesize knowledge and practices." (Crow, ed., 2011, p. 42)

imposter syndrome as an inner voice that we carry around. The voice whispers something like, "I have no idea how it is that I came to be doing what I'm doing but to make sure nobody finds me out I'll keep my understandings and practices as private as possible!" (p. 13). The process of collaborative inquiry engages individuals in sharing practices and learning in collaboration with others while focusing on student learning needs. Through the sharing of practices, individuals begin to abandon a *knowing stance* and adopt a *learning stance*. When debriefing the process, it is important for facilitators to engage individuals in considering the stance in which they approached the work.

The process is driven by practice.

As mentioned earlier, adaptive problems require the people with the problem to do the work of solving it. Through collaborative inquiry, teams investigate problems of practice as they relate to student learning. Professional learning, therefore, occurs within practice. Fullan (2011) noted that we need to "use practice to discover strategies that work" (p. 12) and that it is "about finding and learning from practice that works to solve extremely difficult problems" (p. 17). This is the essence of collaborative inquiry. Furthermore, since learning occurs in context, the dilemma of transferring new skills, knowledge, and competencies is resolved. When debriefing the process, it is important for facilitators to engage individuals in considering how deliberate practice helped deepen their knowledge about improving student learning.

> "Doing is the crucible of change."
> (Fullan, 2011, p. 3)

Actions are informed by evidence.

Actions are informed by evidence when participants are invited to experiment with new strategies and assess the impact of those strategies. Collaborative inquiry requires that individuals use different types of evidence as a basis for considering how teacher actions affect student outcomes. In addition to documenting implementation of the actions identified, teams consider observations, conversations, and/or the examination of student work products including achievement test data. Teams use this evidence to make informed decisions about practice. When the evidence uncovers new knowledge that contradicts participants' current understandings, cognitive dissonance results, leading

> "Evidence of ongoing increases in student learning is a powerful motivator for teachers during the inevitable setbacks that accompany complex change efforts." (Crow, ed., 2011, p. 37)

to new thinking and beliefs. When debriefing the process, it is important for facilitators to engage individuals in considering the degree to which their actions were informed by evidence.

Three activities that facilitators could use to debrief the process are included in the section that follows. The first two (Activity 17 and Activity 18) are designed to use with individual teams. Activity 19 is designed to use with multiple teams. If facilitators are debriefing with a number of teams from one school or a number of teams from across the district, Activity 19 would lend itself to use in this environment.

Activity 17—Along a Continuum

> Materials Needed: Characteristics of Collaborative Inquiry Continuum (Resource J), Characteristics of Collaborative Inquiry–Start–Stop–Continue (Resource K), and Blank Index Cards

Provide one copy of the Characteristics of Collaborative Inquiry Continuum (Resource J) to each team member. Ask individuals to consider the team as a whole and determine where along the continuum she would place the team concerning each statement. Once team members are finished, facilitators lead a discussion regarding strengths and areas for improvement. During the discussion, facilitators record responses on the chart located at the top of the template Characteristics of Collaborative Inquiry—Start—Stop—Continue (Resource K).

Figure 5.1   Characteristics of Collaborative Inquiry Continuum

Select a place along each continuum that you believe best represents your collaborative inquiry team regarding each statement.

Collaborative

1. Norms that enable effective collaboration are in place.

Beginning	Developing	Applying	Innovating

2. When meeting as a learning team, our work together is owned by every member of the team.

Beginning	Developing	Applying	Innovating

3. Decision making authority is dispersed amongst individuals.

Beginning	Developing	Applying	Innovating

Identifying Strengths

Possible Prompts: Quickly review your responses in each of the five areas identified in the Collaborative Inquiry Continuum. In which area do you think our team is strongest? Are we collaborative? Reflective? Do we take a learning stance? Is our process driven by practice? Are our actions informed by evidence?

Identifying Areas for Improvement

Possible Prompts: In which area do you think our team needs to improve? Why?

Next, the facilitator leads the team in a think-pair-share to consider what to start doing, stop doing, and continue doing. Distribute one blank index card per individual. Ask individuals to divide the index card into three columns and record "Start," Stop," and "Continue" at the top of each column.

Possible Prompts: Think (on your own) about what we need to start doing, stop doing, and continue doing—record ideas in each column on your index card.

After a few minutes, ask individuals to pair with one other person on the team to share ideas. Ideas on which partners agree could then be shared with the larger group as the facilitator opens the discussion to the entire team. A template in which to record information gleaned from the team is provided at the bottom of the template Characteristics of Collaborative Inquiry—Start—Stop—Continue (Resource K).

> Facilitators might be interested in documenting changes in culture from one year to another. The continuums contain evidence that might be useful in documenting cultural shifts. Facilitators might gather and store the information for future reference. If so, be sure to let team members know how the information is going to be used and that individuals will remain anonymous (do not ask team members to include their names on the continuums).

Activity 18—Metaphors to Represent Our Learning

Materials Needed: Blank Piece of Paper, Markers or Ballpoint Pens

Metaphors are literary devices used to understand and experience one thing in terms of another. Jensen (2006) noted that metaphors are not "a mere linguistic device for adding color to dialogue" but that they are "salient features of our thinking and our discourse about education" (p. 14). Suggesting that there is a basis for using metaphors to better understand the social contexts of education practice, Jensen (2006) pointed out that metaphors can be a valuable tool for gaining new insights and that they "can be a means through which to see the good, the bad, the positive, the negative, the myths that limit growth, and the ideas that expand possibilities" (p. 13). In this activity, facilitators engage team members in choosing metaphors that, in their opinion, best represent their learning during each of the four stages of collaborative inquiry.

Begin this activity by reviewing the four stages of collaborative inquiry. During Stage 1, teams developed a question about a particular link between professional practice and student results and formulated a theory of action. In Stage 2, teams determined what evidence to collect and developed common understandings of practices. In Stage 3, teams collectively analyzed evidence and formulated conclusions. During Stage 4, teams consolidated their learning by documenting, sharing, and celebrating.

Distribute one sheet of blank paper to each team member and ask participants to fold it twice so that the paper is divided into four sections once it is unfolded. Ask participants to label sections for each stage in the process. Next, ask individuals to consider a metaphor to represent their learning during each stage in the process.

> *Possible Prompts:* Let's start with Stage 1. While we were framing the problem by identifying student learning needs and developing our theory of action, how would you describe your learning? What did you feel and experience from the perspective of a learner? Now think about other things that share some of these qualities and determine a metaphor that would represent your learning during this stage in the process.

Once members of the team have developed metaphors for each stage, invite them to share with the entire group. Based on the sharing, lead a discussion about what the team might do differently while engaging in the process again.

Activity 19—Graffiti

> Materials Needed: Different Color Markers (one color for each role-like group), Chart Paper (with the following questions recorded at the top: How does collaborative inquiry differ from other staff development that you have experienced? What did you learn about data? What did you learn about implementation? What were your challenges? What did you value?)

Facilitators can use this activity with a large group when collaborative inquiry teams from the same or different schools come together for debriefing. Facilitators should consider regrouping members of various teams in like-roles (administrators, coaches, primary teachers, department heads, etc.) for the purpose of this activity. If this is the first time school teams have been brought together, however, facilitators should consider building community prior to regrouping members of individual school teams.

Hang each chart paper (containing one question) in different locations around the room. These locations will serve as "graffiti stations." Divide the audience into role-like groups and provide each group with a different color marker. Assign a graffiti station as the starting point for each group. For example, a group of administrators might begin at Station 1 (How does collaborative inquiry differ from other staff development that you have experienced?), and a group of coaches might begin at Station 2 (What did you learn about data?). For a short period, groups record their graffiti on the chart. After 3 to 5 minutes, stop the groups and ask them to rotate to the next station. Upon arriving at the new station, role-like groups read what was written by the previous group. The new group places a check-mark next to ideas they agree with and a question mark next to ideas that are not clear to them or that they have questions about. They also add new ideas and information to the chart. After a few minutes, the facilitator stops the groups and asks them to rotate a third time, repeating this process until the role-like groups arrive back at their original graffiti station. Once back at their original station, groups read the charts, summarize the ideas, and prepare to present the summary to the entire group. Role-like groups might categorize comments and draw conclusions as part of their presentation. In organizing the large group sharing, it is the responsibility of the facilitator to call on groups and acknowledge the common ideas generated by the discussion.

REFLECTION FOR FACILITATORS

A final set of skills and approaches is offered in Table 5.1. While reflection was an instrumental aspect in adapting to change for team members, it is hoped that facilitators reflected on their practices and experiences as well. One final task suggested is that facilitators review their personal reflections related to the skills and approaches of effective facilitation recorded at the end of each stage and identify their strengths and areas for development.

Table 5.1 Reflection for Facilitators

Facilitator Skills and Approaches	Level 1	Level 2	Level 3	Level 4
Maintains norms	Beginning	Developing	Applying	Innovating
Is a good listener/good questioner	Beginning	Developing	Applying	Innovating
Is assertive about the need for facilitation in effective groups	Beginning	Developing	Applying	Innovating
Helps others assume leadership and facilitation roles	Beginning	Developing	Applying	Innovating
Transparently solicits feedback on facilitation	Beginning	Developing	Applying	Innovating

Source: Adapted from National School Reform Faculty: New York: Facilitation Standards.

Strong professional learning communities produce schools where students are able to meet the high expectations set for them and achieve outcomes that they might not thought possible. By using collaborative inquiry as an approach to professional learning, facilitators assist participants in developing the adaptive capacity to address and overcome difficult problems they face everyday. The ability to address student learning needs no longer depends on individual teachers but on the collective wisdom brought by a team of educators with diverse experiences and expertise. Difficult challenges are met through a coordinated and collective response that helps to ensure greater success for *all* students. Inquiry becomes a broader process to transform the culture of a school.

This book was designed to assist facilitators in guiding teams through the formal process of inquiry. Finally, consider the following: *What might you do differently the next time you facilitate teams through the stages of collaborative inquiry to ensure the work is purposeful, productive, and impactful?*

Resources

Resource A. Identifying Student Learning Needs

Student Learning Needs Based on Common Core State Standards	Student Learning Needs Based on Behaviors and Work Habits
Need: Students need to develop the ability to evaluate other points of view critically and constructively. **Evidence:** They do not question texts and often take material at face value.	**Need:** Students need to stay organized. **Evidence:** They miss important dates and are unable to juggle the demands of multiple courses.
Need: Students need to improve estimation skills. **Evidence:** They cannot "ballpark" reasonable guesses.	**Need:** Students need to complete tasks. **Evidence:** They give up when faced with challenging problems.
Need: Students lack the ability to determine key points from lessons, texts, and videos. **Evidence:** When asked to summarize information students are unable to distinguish important and irrelevant details.	**Need:** Students need to value education. **Evidence:** They lack motivation and interest.
Need: Students have difficulty delineating and evaluating arguments. **Evidence:** They have a difficult time determining sufficiency of evidence in claims.	**Need:** Students need to stay focused. **Evidence:** They tune out halfway through class.
Need: Students need to strengthen their writing. **Evidence:** Conferences with students reveal that they have a difficult time knowing what to revise in their written work.	**Need:** Students need to behave in nonegocentric ways. **Evidence:** They often come to class with a "me-me-me" mentality.

Resource B. Sphere of Concern Versus Realm of Control

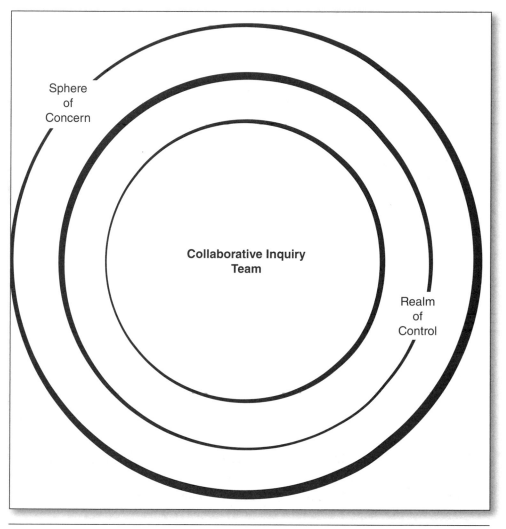

Source: National School Reform Faculty (NSRF). Created by Daniel Baron. Adapted by Jenni Donohoo. http://www.nsrfharmony.org. Reproduced with permission.

Resource C. Examples of Purpose Statements

Student Learning Need—In math, students experience difficulty applying strategies for solving problems.

Problem Framed—Students are able to perform procedures but lack conceptual understanding needed to apply learning to new and different situations when solving problems.

Purpose Statement—The purpose of this inquiry is to understand how to develop Grade 7 students' conceptual understanding of measurement.

Student Learning Need—Students lack the ability to transfer their learning by applying strategies in different contexts.

Problem Framed—Students don't automatically use visual representations (e.g., charts and graphs) to communicate their understanding in subjects other than mathematics.

Purpose Statement—The purpose of this inquiry is to explore how to assist students in the intermediate division in transferring strategies across content areas.

Student Learning Need—Students have difficulty making inferences from text.

Problem Framed—Students are able to answer questions where information is explicitly stated in the text but have a difficult time "reading between the lines."

Purpose Statement—The purpose of this inquiry is to identify practices that will assist students in identifying implicitly stated information in texts.

Student Learning Need—Students have difficulty critically analyzing material and considering bias.

Problem Framed—Students accept what they read at face value and do not consider the author and/or source of the material.

Purpose Statement—The purpose of this inquiry is to discover how to help students in the 10th grade identify bias in historical documents and use that information to identify their own biases.

Student Learning Need—Students lack the skills of argumentation along with the dispositions required to engage in courteous discourse.

Problem Framed—When working in groups, students lack the ability to debate skillfully and respectfully.

Purpose Statement—The purpose of this inquiry is to discover ways to facilitate productive group work focused on the skills of argumentation in senior-level classes.

Student Learning Need: Students have difficulty making connections between what is taught and the real world.

Problem Framed: Students often fail to see the relevance or purpose in content being presented in classrooms.

Purpose Statement: The purpose of this inquiry is to discover how to establish relevance and purpose so that students make better connections between what they are learning in school and the world around them.

Student Learning Need: Students experience difficulty summarizing material and identifying important information for note-taking purposes.

Problem Framed: Students lack the skills necessary to extract main points from printed text and classroom lectures.

Purpose Statement: The purpose of this inquiry is to understand how to best support students in gaining skills needed to summarize materials in history classes.

Resource D. Inquiry Questions—Examples—Strong and Weak

1. How can we implement more effective note-taking strategies to support students in understanding and retaining information?

2. Does a sense of belonging affect academic achievement?

3. Will the use of metacognitive strategies increase students' ability to self-regulate?

4. What impact does allowing students multiple opportunities to demonstrate what they know and can do have on student learning?

5. What impact does the use of exit cards have on students' ability to identify essential understandings in a lesson/unit?

6. Will listening to students give us a better understanding of their needs?

7. What impact does students moderating work have on their ability to understand and use assessment criteria?

8. Does increased collaboration lead to increased student achievement?

9. Can we promote student self-assessment through guided reading instruction and independent reading opportunities?

10. What impact does the use of manipulatives have on students' ability to solve problems in mathematics class?

11. What is the impact of content-area teachers explicitly teaching how to write an opinion on students' ability to form and support an opinion?

12. Can asking essential questions affect student motivation?

13. Can social networking be used to motivate students and parents to engage in the learning process thereby favorably affecting levels of achievement?

14. Has student achievement increased as the result of technology being integrated into the classroom?

15. How can we implement assessment *as* learning strategies to support students' ability to monitor their understanding?

16. How does elimination of number grades throughout the year (with the exception of end-of-term/semester grades) impact students' attitudes?

Answer Key

Examples of Strong Questions

Questions 1, 4, 5, 7, 10, 11, 15, and 16 are examples of strong questions. These questions begin with the words *how* or *what*. They are exploratory in nature (e.g., exploring an impact) and therefore, do not assume a causal relationship between two variables. Each of the questions identifies a practice (e.g., note-taking strategies, exit cards, use of manipulatives) and a student learning outcome (e.g., form and support opinions, retain information, identify essential understandings).

Examples of Weak Questions

Questions 2, 3, 6, 8, 9, 12, 13, and 14 are examples of weaker questions. These questions begin with the words *has, can, does,* and *will*. They can be answered with a simple yes or no. Some of the questions are worded in a way that assumes causality (e.g., increased collaboration = increased student achievement).

Resource E. Theory of Action T-Chart

If . . . (Action)	Then . . . (Outcome)

Resource F. Innovation Configuration Map Template

Component 1				

Component 2				

Component 3				

(Continued)

(Continued)

Component 4				
Component 5				
Component 6				

Source: Richardson, J. (2004). Taking measure: Innovation configurations gauge the progress of a new initiative. *Tools for Schools.* National Staff Development Council, Oxford, OH. Reprinted with permission.

Resource G. Data Collection Plan Template

Inquiry Question: _____

What evidence is going to be collected?	How is the evidence going to be collected?	When is the evidence going to be collected? By whom?
Data Source 1 (related to the student learning need identified)		
Data Source 2 (related to the student learning need identified)		
Data Source 3 (related to the student learning need identified)		

Evidence of Implementation of Practice:

Resource H. Levels of Implementation Templates

Levels of Implementation Template (Classroom)

What does deep implementation of _____ look like in the classroom?

Beginning Level	Developing Level	Applying Level	Innovating Level

Reflect on the level of implementation in your classroom. Where along the continuum are you?

Resource H. Levels of Implementation Templates (Continued)

Levels of Implementation Template (Collaborative Inquiry Team)

What does deep implementation of _____ look like within your collaborative inquiry team?

Beginning Level	Developing Level	Applying Level	Innovating Level

Reflect on the level of implementation regarding your collaborative inquiry team. Where along the continuum is the team?

Resource H. Levels of Implementation Templates (Continued)

Levels of Implementation Template (Entire Staff)

What does deep implementation of _____ look like for the entire staff?

Beginning Level	Developing Level	Applying Level	Innovating Level

Reflect on the level of implementation for the entire staff. Where along the continuum is the staff as a whole?

Resource I. Collaborative Inquiry Teams—Small Group Sharing

Roles

Table Facilitator—coaches, consultants, or volunteer at the table

Presenter(s)—each team will have an opportunity to present

Recorder(s)—pair or individual on the presenter's left records

Participants—make comments and ask questions during presentations

Preparation

1. *Identify/Select a Table Facilitator.* There are 10 minutes allotted for each collaborative inquiry team. It is the Table Facilitator's responsibility to ensure that the group adheres to the timelines. Table Facilitators should prompt the discussion accordingly. Note for the Table Facilitator: The following is a suggested structure. If this format does not suit the group, please feel free to adapt it at any time. In an effort to honor everyone's learning and work, please ensure that each school team has equal time to share.

2. *Determine which team will present first.* Request that the team to the presenter's left records comments and questions (Step 2). These notes will be given to presenters when their sharing is complete.

Step 1: Overview of the Inquiry (4 minutes)

The presenting team provides an overview of their collaborative inquiry.

The presenting team might consider the following prompts to guide their sharing.

Our collaborative inquiry was about...	Our most valuable lesson/learning occurred when...
It involved us...	We found out...
It was prompted because...	We still do not know...
We felt it was important because...	We are still puzzled about...
We believed...(theory of action)	We recommend...
	Our next steps are...

Step 2: Comments, Questions, and Answers (4 minutes)

The participants in the group have an opportunity to comment and ask questions of the presenting team. The presenters comment on the comments and answer the questions as they are posed. Questions should get to the heart of the presenter's experience and learning. Ideally, questions will provoke deeper thought and allow the presenter to consider different avenues or alternative scenarios. The intent here is that the questions asked may not have correct answers. Correctness may be based on logical projections, contextual, or arrived at through inference. They may sound like the following:

What may have happened if . . .

What might you have tried instead . . .

What would you do the next time . . .

How are you going to . . .

Was there anything else you could have used . . .

How will you know next time . . .

Step 3: Reflection (2 minutes)

The presenting team has two minutes to share any additional reflections based on comments and questions that arose.

The team to the left shares the comments and questions with the presentation team.

Repeat the process until each school team has had an opportunity to share.

Resource J. Characteristics of Collaborative Inquiry Continuum

Select a place along each continuum that you believe best represents your collaborative inquiry team regarding each statement.

Collaborative

1. Norms that enable effective collaboration are in place.

Beginning	Developing	Applying	Innovating

2. When meeting as a learning team, our work together is owned by every member of the team.

Beginning	Developing	Applying	Innovating

3. Decision making authority is dispersed among individuals.

Beginning	Developing	Applying	Innovating

4. Diversity of opinion is promoted and evident in our joint work.

Beginning	Developing	Applying	Innovating

Reflective

5. Routines that encourage and enable individuals to consider and reflect on solutions to their problems of practice are in place.

Beginning	Developing	Applying	Innovating

6. Group members consistently use data to self-assess and reflect.

Beginning	Developing	Applying	Innovating

7. Team members are experimenting with new teaching ideas in the classroom and reflecting on how well they are working.

Beginning	Developing	Applying	Innovating

8. Thinking is more intentional and explicit based on reflection.

Beginning	Developing	Applying	Innovating

Learning Stance

9. Team members not only promote but fully participate in each stage of the collaborative inquiry cycle.

Beginning	Developing	Applying	Innovating

10. Our time together is focused on student learning, professional learning, teaching practice, and/or leading.

Beginning	Developing	Applying	Innovating

11. Team members are open to new ideas and actively seek new information from relevant sources to help inform next steps.

Beginning	Developing	Applying	Innovating

12. Team members find value in the process.

Beginning	Developing	Applying	Innovating

Process Driven by Practice

13. Our work involves examining our own and each other's practice.

Beginning	Developing	Applying	Innovating

14. We use practice to discover strategies that work.

Beginning	Developing	Applying	Innovating

15. We draw on outside ideas in relation to how they relate to our situation.

Beginning	Developing	Applying	Innovating

16. Work is connected to and impacting the work of the professional learning community and wider school improvement efforts.

Beginning	Developing	Applying	Innovating

Actions Informed by Evidence

17. Analysis of relevant and current data is deemed important and is an ongoing priority for the team.

Beginning	Developing	Applying	Innovating

18. The team considers teaching practices (in light of student data) and determines approaches that are successful and those that need to be changed.

Beginning	Developing	Applying	Innovating

19. The team considers multiple sources of evidence to gain a well-rounded picture of their inquiry.

Beginning	Developing	Applying	Innovating

20. Current student learning data is collaboratively examined and provides a basis for considering next steps for the team's inquiry.

Beginning	Developing	Applying	Innovating

Resource K. Characteristics of Collaborative Inquiry—Start—Stop—Continue

Based on the responses from the Characteristics of Collaborative Inquiry Continuums, record the strengths and areas for improvement identified by the team.

Strengths	Areas for Improvement

Based on information in the previous chart, what might the team start doing, stop doing, and continue doing?

Start

Stop

Continue

References

Argyris, C. (1999). *On organizational learning* (2nd ed.). Malden, MA: Blackwell.

Argyris, C. & Schon, D. (1974). *Theory in practice: Increasing professional effectiveness.* San Francisco, CA: Jossey-Bass.

Bennett, B. (2011). Instruction: A few thinks. *The SDCO Connection, 2*(3), 12–15.

Bernhardt, V. (2000).Intersections: New routes open when one type of data crosses another. *Journal of Staff Development, 21*(1), 33–36.

Bernhardt, V. (n.d.). Measuring school processes. *Education for the future.* Retrieved from http://eff.csuchico.edu/downloads/MeasuringProcesses.pdf

Bushe, G. (2010). *Clear leadership: Sustaining real collaboration and partnership at work* (revised ed.). Boston, MA: Davis-Black.

City, E., Elmore, R., Fiarman, S., & Teitel, L. (2009). *Instructional rounds in education: A network approach to improving teaching and learning.* Cambridge, MA: Harvard Education Press.

Creswell, J. (2002). *Educational research: Planning, conducting and evaluating quantitative and qualitative research.* Upper Saddle River, NJ: Merrill Prentice Hall.

Crow, T. (Ed). (2011). *Standards for professional learning.* Oxford, OH: Learning Forward.

Donohoo, J. (2012). Five effective steps: Supporting our teachers in implementing change. Ontario Principals' Council. *The Register.*

DuFour, R. (1998). Why celebrate? It sends a vivid message about what is valued. *Journal of Staff Development, 19*(4), 58–59.

DuFour, R., DuFour, R., Eaker, R., & Karhanek, G. (2010). *Raising the bar and closing the gap: Whatever it takes.* Bloomington, IN: Solution Tree Press.

Earl, L. (2003). *Assessment as learning: Using classroom assessment to maximize student learning.* Thousand Oaks, CA: Corwin.

Earl, L., & Katz, S. (2006). *Leading schools in a data-rich world: Harnessing data for school improvement.* Thousand Oaks, CA: Corwin.

Easton, L. (Ed.). (2008). *Powerful designs for professional learning* (2nd ed.). Oxford, OH: National Staff Development Council.

Fullan, M. (2006). Leading professional learning. *The School Administrator,* 10–14.

Fullan, M. (2008). *The six secrets of change: What the best leaders do to help their organizations survive and thrive.* San Francisco, CA: Jossey-Bass.

Fullan, M. (2011). *Change leader: Learning to do what matters most.* San Francisco, CA: Jossey-Bass.

Fullan, M., Hill, P., & Crévola, C. (2006). *Breakthrough.* Thousand Oaks, CA: Corwin.

Fullan, M., & Sharratt, L. (2007). Sustaining leadership in complex times: An individual and system solution. In Brent Davis (Ed.), *Developing Sustainable Leadership* (p. 116–136). London, England: Sage.

Gawande, A. (2009). *The checklist manifesto: How to get things right.* New York, NY: Metropolitan Books.

Gersten, R., Vaughn, S., Deshler, D., & Schiller, E. (1997). What we know about using research findings: Implications for improving special education practice. *Journal of Learning Disabilities, 30*(5), 466–476.

Guskey, T. (2000). *Evaluating professional development.* Thousand Oaks, CA: Corwin.

Guskey, T. (2006). A conversation with Thomas R. Guskey. *Evaluation Exchange: A Periodical on Emerging Strategies in Evaluation, XI*(4).

Hall, G., & Hord, S. (2006). *Implementing change: Patterns, principles, and potholes* (2nd ed.). Boston, MA: Pearson Education.

Halton, N., & Smith, D. (1995). Reflection in teacher education: Towards definition and implementation. *Teaching and Teacher Education, 11*(1), 33–49.

Hargreaves, A. & Fullan, M. (2012). *Professional capital: Transforming teaching in every school.* New York, NY: Teachers' College Press.

Hattie, J. (2009). *Visible learning: A synthesis of over 800 meta-analyses relating to achievement.* New York, NY: Routledge.

Hattie, J. (2012). *Visible learning for teachers: Maximizing impact on learning.* New York, NY: Routledge.

Heath, D., & Heath, C. (2010). *Switch: How to change things when change is hard.* New York, NY: Random House.

Heifetz, R. (1994). *Leadership without easy answers.* Cambridge, MA: Harvard Press.

Heifetz, R., Grashow, A., & Linsky, M. (2009). *The practice of adaptive leadership: Tools and tactics for changing your organization and the world.* Boston, MA: Harvard Business Press.

Hirsh, S., & Killion, J. (2007). *The learning educator: A new era for professional learning.* Oxford, OH: National Staff Development Council.

Hord, S. (2008). Evolution of the professional learning community. *Journal of Staff Development, 29*(3), 10–13.

Huffman, J. (2001). *The role of shared values and vision in creating professional learning communities.* Austin, TX: Southwestern Educational Development Lab.

Jensen, D. (2006). Metaphors as a bridge to understanding educational and social contexts. *International Journal of Qualitative Methods, 5*(1), 1–17.

Joyce, B., Showers, B., & Rolheiser-Bennett, C. (1987). Staff development and student learning: A synthesis of research on models of teaching. *Educational Leadership, 45*(2),11–23.

Katz, S. (2010). Together is better . . . sometimes: Building and sustaining impactful learning communities within and across schools. *The SDCO Connection, 1*(3), 12–13.

Katz, S., Earl, L., & Ben Jaafar, S. (2009). *Building and connecting learning communities: The power of networks for school improvement.* Thousand Oaks, CA: Corwin.

Killion, J., Hord, S., Roy, P., Kennedy, J., & Hirsh, S. (2012). *Standards into practice: School-based roles–Innovation configuration maps for standards for professional learning.* Oxford, OH: Learning Forward.

Knight, J. (2007). Five key points to building a coaching program. *Journal of Staff Development, 28*(1), 26–31.

Knight, J. (2009). Coaching: The key to translating research into practice lies in continuous, job-embedded learning with ongoing support. *Journal of Staff Development, 30*(1), 18–22.

Lee, I. (2009). Ten mismatches between teachers' beliefs and written feedback practice. *ELT Journal, 63*(1).

Levin, B. (2008). *How to change 5000 schools: A practical and positive approach for leading change at every level.* Cambridge, MA: Harvard Education Press.

Lieberman, A., & Miller, A. (2004). *Teacher leadership.* San Francisco, CA: Jossey-Bass.

MacDonald, E. (2011). When nice won't suffice: Honest discourse is key to shifting school culture. *Journal of Staff Development, 32*(3), 45–51.

Marzano, R. (2003). *What works in schools: Translating research into action.* Alexandria, VA: Association for Supervision and Curriculum Development.

Marzano, R. (2011). Art and science of teaching: It's how you use a strategy. *Educational Leadership, 69*(4), 88–89.

Marzano, R. Waters, T., & McNulty, B. (2005). *School leadership that works: From research to results.* Alexandria, VA: Association for Supervision and Curriculum Development.

Ministry of Education, Ontatrio. (2010). *Growing success: Assessment, evaluation, and reporting in Ontario schools,* (1st ed.). Queen's Printer for Ontario.

Mitchell, C., & Sackney, L. (2009). *Sustainable improvement: Building learning communities that endure.* Rotterdam, Netherlands: Sense Publishers.

Murray, S., Ma, X., & Mazur, J. (2009). Effects of peer coaching on teachers' collaborative interactions and students' mathematical achievement. *The Journal of Educational Research, 102*(3), 203–212.

National School Reform Faculty. (n.d). NSRF materials. Retrieved from http://www.nsrfharmony.org/protocol/a_z.html

National Staff Development Council's Standards for Staff Development. (2001). Oxford, OH: Author.

Organization Unbound. (n.d.). Retrieved from http://organizationunbound.org/the-learning-stance-by-anthi-theiopoulou

Reeves, D. (2008). *Reframing teacher leadership to improve your school.* Alexandria, VA: Association for Supervision and Curriculum Development.

Reeves, D. (2009). *Leading change in your school: How to conquer myths, build commitment, and get results.* Alexandria, VA: Association for Supervision and Curriculum Development.

Reeves, D. (2010). *Transforming professional development into student results.* Alexandria, VA: Association for Supervision and Curriculum Development.

Richardson, J. (2004). Taking measure: Innovation Configurations gauge the progress of a new initiative. *Tools for Schools.* Oxford, OH: National Staff Development Council.

Robinson, V., Lloyd, C., & Rowe, K. (2008). The impact of leadership on student outcomes: An analysis of the differential effects of leadership types. *Educational Administration Quarterly, 44*(5), 635–674.

Senge, P. M. (1990). *The fifth discipline: The art and practice of the learning organization.* New York, NY: Doubleday.

Senge, P., Scharmer, C. O., Jaworski, J., & Flowers, B. (2004). *Presence: An exploration of profound change in people, organizations, and society.* New York, NY: Doubleday.

Sinek, S. (2009). *Start with why: How great leaders inspire everyone to take action.* New York, NY: Penguin Group.

Stoll, L. (2010). Connecting learning communities: Capacity building for systemic change. In Hargreaves, A., Lieberman, A., Fullan, M., & Hopkins, D. (Eds.), *Second international handbook of educational change, Part 1* (pp. 468–484). New York, NY: Springer.

Supovitz, J. (2006). *The case for district-based reform: Leading, building, and sustaining school improvement.* Cambridge, MA: Harvard University Press.

Vander Ark, T. (2006). *Change leadership: A practical guide to transforming our schools.* San Francisco, CA: Jossey-Bass.

Index

CORWIN

A SAGE Company

The Corwin logo—a raven striding across an open book—represents the union of courage and learning. Corwin is committed to improving education for all learners by publishing books and other professional development resources for those serving the field of PreK–12 education. By providing practical, hands-on materials, Corwin continues to carry out the promise of its motto: **"Helping Educators Do Their Work Better."**